Graduate with Zero Debt: How to Finish College Without Student Loans

by Pallas Snider Ziporyn

PALTA BOOKS

Graduate with Zero Debt:
How to Finish College Without Student Loans
Pallas Snider Ziporyn
Published by Palta Books
Copyright 2015 Pallas Snider Ziporyn
Book cover design by James, GoOnWrite.com
ISBN: 978-0-9913137-7-8

Discover Other Titles by Pallas Snider Ziporyn:
The International Student's Guide to American Colleges

Table of Contents

Resources..................149

The Basics

Introduction

College today is more expensive today than at any other point in the country's history. The average college student in the United States graduates with approximately $30,000 in debt, and it is not uncommon to find students graduating with debt approaching the six figure mark. The price of college has been increasing faster than the rate of inflation which means that college today costs approximately four times more than it did just a few decades ago.

Talking about the numbers can sound boring and pointless. The costs are what they are, and college is an essential, so we should just live with it, right? I wrote this book because I believe there is a way for every kind of student to graduate without the burden of massive debt. And I'll try not to be boring as I explain to you how. I want to help you graduate debt free because there is nothing more boring (and tedious) than analyzing interest on your monthly loan payments, and there are very few things more frustrating than having to stay at a job you hate because of astronomical student loan debt.

I have to admit that when I was in high school, I didn't really understand much about student loans or the burden they imposed. Sure, I knew that $30,000 or more was a lot of money, but I didn't have a good sense of what it would mean to pay off that sort of a sum. I was fortunate. I graduated from college without any debt. My husband, however, was not so lucky. He attended the college of his dreams, a small liberal arts college with a high price tag. They offered him substantial financial aid but like at most colleges, that financial aid package included a substantial amount of loans.

At the time, he didn't think much of it. This was his education, right? Going to a prestigious school where you could gain a liberal arts education would be priceless. At least that was what we had always been told. I once heard a student say, "My education is priceless, but at the same time, there is a price." There was a price to my husband's education. It was $75,000 in loans that we got to start paying off in $850 monthly increments nine months after he graduated. It had never occurred to me until we started paying off those monthly bills that it perhaps wasn't worth it. My husband had a wonderful college experience, and it was transformative in many ways. However, when we were forced to both work jobs we disliked after graduation in order to make our loan payments, and we still had to pay for everything else in life (rent, food, car, etc.), it made us rethink things.

If my husband had realized at age 18 what having student debt meant, he would have likely done things differently. There were ways he could have saved if he had known about them then. Yes, he could have picked a different school, perhaps a state school where the tuition was less. He could have applied for scholarships. He could have taken a gap year, negotiated more with the financial aid office, or even taken more internships during his time in college. Any of these solutions would have significantly reduced his debt burden, and by the time he graduated, our debt load could have been significantly reduced or even eliminated.

If you have picked up this book, you are far ahead of many of your peers who will sign away on a loan without thinking twice and not realize what they've gotten themselves into until their senior year of college when the reality of the looming payments smacks them in the face. You don't have to be in that situation. You don't have to compromise your life after college in order to have a great college experience now. If you think ahead, and you do your planning, you can graduate from college debt free or at least close.

I've compiled this guide to give you the tools to help you figure out how to make your dream of graduating debt free of reality. I am not prescribing a one size fits all solution. You may be set on going to a private school. You might dream of majoring in English. You might be certain that you want to spend the full four years of college instead of graduating early after three. There is more than one way to graduate without crippling student loans, and we are going to explore many of the options so that you can figure out which works best for you and the vision you have of your life.

This book is divided into three sections. In the next few chapters, we'll cover the basics of the American financial aid system. Then, we'll go over specific strategies you might take in order to reduce or eliminate your debt load. We'll review sixteen unique strategies each of which can save you thousands and discuss which strategies might be best for you based on your academic record and financial situation. Whether you are a top student or are just scraping by and whether your family's income is below the poverty line or well into the six digits, there are strategies in this section that will save you money. In the third section, you'll find a list of resources that will help you in your quest to eliminate loans. You can use this section to find the best in-state tuition rates, a list of where you can get out-of-state tuition waivers, over a hundred full tuition scholarships, and dozens of outside scholarships for essays, academic achievement, leadership, artistic ability, and other criteria.

We need to be honest. Graduating debt free is not going to be easy. If you are committed to this goal you are going to have to work hard. There will likely be essays to write, forms to fill out, and many people to call. The system unfortunately is not set up to make having an affordable college experience automatic. That said, if you believe in this vision strongly enough, and you put in the work, the suggestions in this book can end up saving you thousands of dollars. And though the process of getting there might be boring and even tedious at times, when you graduate and have the freedom to spend the year abroad, take your dream job, or even buy your first condo or house by the time you are thirty, you'll be glad you made the effort.

Chapter 1
How to Apply for Financial Aid

We're going to start with the basics: how to apply for financial aid. The mechanics of applying for aid are not fun, but if you want free money, they are necessary steps. We'll go through this quickly but we'll cover all the key points you need to know.

<u>The FAFSA</u>

If you are hoping to receive federal student aid (or even institutional aid at most schools), you will need to fill out a form put out by the federal government called the Free Application for Federal Student Aid (FAFSA). You are eligible to fill out receive aid via the FAFSA if you meet the following criteria:

•   Are registered with the Selective Service System (for conscription) if you are required to do so (males between 18 and 25)
•   Have US Citizenship, are a US national, or eligible non-citizen
•   Have a valid Social Security number
•   Have a high school diploma, GED, or by gaining a high school education through a home school setting as approved by state law
•   Plan to enroll as a regular student in an eligible degree or certificate program

- Don't owe refunds on federal student grants
- Are not in default on any student loans

The good news is that as it says in its name, filling out the FAFSA is free. The bad news is that it is a pain to fill out, and you are required to do the thing before every year of college in order to continue to receive aid.

You can fill out the form online, but if you prefer to do the paper application, that is still an option. The form becomes available January 1st before each academic year, and the earlier you fill it out, the better as most aid is awarded on a first come, first serve basis.

In order to fill out the form, your family will need to collect information about their income, assets, and taxes. You can use the IRS Data Retrieval Tool (http://www.irsdataretrievaltool.com) to get information regarding taxes which is what the US Department of Education recommends.

You can complete the FAFSA directly through the US Department of Education either on FAFSA.gov or by downloading and mailing it in. If you do things this way, the whole process is free as it was originally intended to be. But because many people find the questions on the form complex and confusing, some students opt to use a fee-based FAFSA preparation service to help them gather the appropriate information. The average family spends approximately 78 minutes filling out the FAFSA. Using one of these services can help you get through the process in under 30 minutes. Furthermore, using one of these services will help you make sure you don't make common mistakes such as miscalculating your adjusted gross income, or listing your primary residence as an asset. Ultimately, avoiding these kinds of mistakes may more than make up for the cost of using a service by increasing your aid package.

It is up to you whether you think using a fee-based service is worthwhile. With the wealth of free information available on how to fill out the FAFSA via the internet, you should be able to fill out the form just fine on your own with a bit of research. If the FAFSA's 130 questions intimidate you, however, a fee-based service may help calm your nerves and complete the form quickly, which as we discussed helps put you in the first come, first serve line for aid faster.

<u>College List on the FAFSA</u>

You'll notice that the FAFSA asks you to list up to ten colleges where you are applying. This list has been somewhat controversial because individual colleges can see this list when they receive your completed FAFSA form. Some colleges have been criticized for using the the order in which students list the colleges on the FAFSA to affect admissions decisions. Some college admissions officers believe a higher position on this list indicates a stronger student interest in attending their school. In order to keep up matriculation rates, some colleges will favor students who list their school near the top of the FAFSA list more highly than similarly qualified students who list their school further down. While the extent of this practice is disputed (and many schools do not engage in this practice), the best policy is to list the schools on your FAFSA alphabetically so the list is less likely to be interpreted as preferential.

The CSS Profile

In addition to the FAFSA, several hundred schools (you can find a list at http://professionals.collegeboard.com/profdownload/PROFILE_Student_Guide.pdf) require you to fill out the CSS Profile (https://student.collegeboard.org/css-financial-aid-profile) in order to receive aid. Administered by the College Board, the CSS Profile is designed to give colleges a more detailed look at your family's finances to help them make a determination of how much institutional aid they will offer you. Although filling out yet another long form is annoying, the schools that use the CSS Profile tend to offer generous institutional aid so the effort you put into filling it out will hopefully be well worth it.

Like the FAFSA, you can fill this form out either on paper or online. Unlike the FAFSA which is a standardized form, the CSS Profile has customized questions specific to the schools on your list. In general, however, you will want to make sure you have detailed information about your family members' salary, dividends, interest income, taxes, and the value of savings and investments.

There is a small fee associated with the CSS Profile which must be paid for each school where it is submitted. Based on the information you fill out in your CSS Profile, you may be granted a fee waiver that would allow you to submit this form without a fee.

With all things financial aid, the earlier you fill things out, the better. Each school will have its own specific deadlines, but trying to get everything done during January of the year you plan to enroll will put you in the best position to receive optimal aid.

Key Points

• Make sure to fill to fill out and submit the FAFSA. The earlier you do this (beginning in January of your senior year), the better.

• You may want to consider a fee-based service to help you fill out the FAFSA completely or accurately. If you decide not to, make sure to do your research first. Mistakes equal lost money.

• Check to see if any of the colleges on your list also require you to submit the CSS Profile.

Chapter 2
Anatomy of a Financial Aid Package

After you submit the FAFSA and/or CSS Profile, you can't do anything but wait until you receive your award letter. The moment you get your financial aid award letter may very well be nearly as exciting as the moment you get your acceptance letter. Usually sent out in mid-April of your senior year (provided that you've submitted your FAFSA by your college's deadline), the award letter will lay out exactly how a college expects you to pay for your first year of college. Most award letters will be broken down into the following categories:

<u>Grants</u>

Grants are money that you don't have to pay back, usually given based on need. You can view these as a gift. Some come directly from the school (institutional grants) and others come from the government such as the Federal Pell Grant, Federal Supplemental Educational Opportunity Grant (FSEOG), and state-sponsored grants. Understanding the grants in your award letter can be confusing because there are many different sources for grants, and you may find that there are many different types of grants listed. The main thing to keep in mind is that if it says the word "grant" it means you are getting free money that never has to be paid back.

Scholarships

Scholarships are another form of money that you are not expected to pay back, offered to you as an award either directly through your college or from an outside source. Unlike grants, which are awarded based on need, scholarships are typically awarded based on academic merit, sports, artistic ability, an essay, heritage, military affiliation, or other factors as determined by each scholarship program. Some scholarships are offered through independent organizations such as a company, foundation, or non-profit and can be applied to any college you decide to attend. Others are specific to a particular institution. Of scholarships specific to an institution, some require a separate application process from that of the college and others use your application for admission to determine your eligibility for a scholarship award. Scholarships are one of the best ways to get money for college because there is ample scholarship money available and lots of money is awarded each year. We will discuss scholarships and where you can find out about them in the coming chapters.

Work-Study

Most financial aid packages will include a line item for work-study which is money that you are expected to earn by working either at an on-campus job or and off-campus job at a private non-profit or public agency. Most schools will offer a number of job offerings that will meet the work-study requirement including more menial jobs such as working in the dining halls or library as well as research assistant jobs or other types of work that are more related to your course study. Keep in mind that these are not full-time jobs. The exact number of hours you will devote to a work-study job will depend upon the school you attend and the job you select, but most work-study jobs will not require (and in many cases not even allow) you to work more than 15-20 hours per week.

Expected Family Contribution (EFC)

Your family contribution is the amount of money your family will need to contribute to your education each year as determined by the college. When you submit the FAFSA, a Student Aid Report will be generated and sent to both you and the colleges you indicate on your form. Part of this report includes what is referred to as the Expected Family Contribution (EFC). The EFC is calculated using a specific formula determined by the federal government. This number takes into account your family's total income (both taxed and untaxed), assets (including home equity, savings, stock holdings, and family-owned businesses), benefits, family size, and number of family members who are planning to attend college in the coming year. The resulting number will determine your eligibility for federal aid programs. This number represents the minimum amount of money a college will expect your family to contribute to your eduction, but it will not necessarily be the actual number you contribute. In most cases, the actual number will end up being higher. However, if you are able to secure a significant number of scholarships, enough to cover above your full need amount, the amount your family actually ends up paying may end up being less than your EFC. We're going to talk about some strategies that will help you do that later in this guide.

There are many online calculators that will help you figure out your EFC, but keep in mind the actual amount your family will be expected to pay will vary significantly from school to school. The only way to really know how much your family will need to pay is to see what it says once you get your award letter.

Federal Loans

When the government offers you federal loans, a standard part of any financial aid package, you are expected to begin paying them back after graduation with interest. Loans are the scariest part of a financial aid package because once you add in the interest, the amount of your loan will balloon over time into a much higher amount than what initially appears. A $5,000 loan at a 5.6% interest rate, for example, will end up generating over $3,000 in interest alone (a whopping 60% of the principal) over a 20-year payoff period.

If you do end up needing some loans in your financial aid package, however, keep in mind that not all loans are created equal. Federal loans, which are administered by the Federal Student Aid Program, in general, are far better than private loans, and of public loans, some are better than others.

The two most common loan types are the Federal Stafford Loans and Perkins loans, both of which are public loans distributed through the Federal Student Aid Program. As a student, you take these loans directly and are legally liable for paying them back. The government also offers PLUS loans which are loans to your parents and are an optional addition to a standard aid package which can help cover unmet need or reduce your family contribution.

Federal Stafford Loans

These are loans administered by the federal government which come in two forms, subsidized and unsubsidized. Subsidized are where the government pays the interest while you are in school, during deferment, and during any grace periods. Unsubsidized loans require you to pay for all of the interest regardless of when it accrued. Which type of Stafford loan you are offered will be determined by your financial need. First-year college students are eligible for up to $5,500 in Stafford loans although this number increases during subsequent years of study. Over four years, you are eligible to take out up to $31,000 in total Stafford loans of which $23,000 can be subsidized.

Perkins Loans

These are low-interest loans (5%) administered by campuses that participate in the program. They are capped at $4,000 annually.

If you have to take out any loans, Stafford Loans and Perkins Loans are the best kinds. Because they are administered by the federal government, they typically have lower interest rates than private loans, are more highly regulated and flexible when it comes to repayment plans and loan deferment. These two types of loans are standard to most need-based financial aid packages although the specific amounts awarded and whether the offer is unsubsidized or subsidized varies.

PLUS Loans

These are federally-administered loans which can be taken out by the parents of dependent undergraduate students who are not determined to have an adverse credit history. These loans are in a parent's name and stay with the parent even after graduation; they cannot be transferred to the child. There is a loan fee to take out these loans (currently 4.292%) and a significant interest rate (which varies depending on when the loan was originated but is currently set to 7.21%). The loans can cover up to the full cost of attendance minus other aid received.

PLUS loans are designed as an extra tool available to students to help them pay for college if their parents want to contribute more than they can afford to pay in cash. They are not a standard part of an aid package (although many parents do end up using them). If they appear on your financial aid award, it should be because either you or your parents requested that any unmet need/the family contribution be covered by PLUS loans. Unfortunately, some colleges automatically put PLUS loans into an aid package as a way to hide unmet need. If you see a PLUS loan on your package, and you didn't request it, it means that the college wasn't able to cover all of your need with the standard arsenal of aid tools (grants, scholarships, Perkins and Stafford loans, EFC, and work-study) and decided to allocate some or all of the shortfall into a PLUS loan. If you notice this on your award letter, keep in mind that you are by no means required to take out the PLUS loan. Your parents could squeeze out extra cash beyond the EFC if they can afford it, you could take out private loans (although generally PLUS loans are preferable), or you could apply for outside scholarships that will reduce these loans.

Unmet Need

What colleges do when determining your aid package is to first take your EFC and subtract it from their total cost of attendance to determine your need. Colleges will then try to meet this need by offering you a mix of grants, federal loans, and work-study to cover as much of the need as they can. Unfortunately, only a small percentage of colleges can actually meet your full need through these means (you can find a list of these schools in Chapter 18). Many schools will max out your federal loans and work-study, offer you the maximum they can offer in institutional grants and/or scholarships, and add in your EFC, and there will still be a shortfall in cash required between your award and the total cost of attendance. When this happens, it is called having unmet need. Essentially, there is not enough money available from all sources for you to pay for your necessary expenses. As a result, your family will be responsible for figuring out how to cover the shortfall. This might mean that your family will need to pay funds out of pocket above the EFC. Or, your parents can decide to take out a PLUS loan or you can take out private student loans. Colleges are often embarrassed to admit that many of their students have unmet need, and so they make it difficult for students to identify it in their award letters. While some schools come right out and have an "unmet need" section of the letter, other schools will automatically allocate unmet funds to PLUS loans or private loans on the award package. If you see that there are any PLUS loans in your aid package, any loans that are not awarded through the federal aid program (either institutional loans or private loans), or if your family contribution section indicates a number higher than your EFC, it means that you have unmet need.

Private Loans

Private loans are administered through a private lending organization. While all loans are best avoided, private students loans are the ones you most need to watch out for. Private student loans typically have higher interest rates than federal loans. While the federal loan interest rate is fixed, the private interest rate is not, and as a result, most private loans are offered at a substantially higher rate than their federal loan counterparts. Furthermore, private loans have fewer repayment options. While federal loans often allow you to choose your payback time horizon, defer interest accumulation during your education or while taking certain kinds of jobs, and even have a portion of your loans forgiven if you pursue certain types of careers, most private loans will not give you this flexibility. As a result $10,000 in private loans ends up being a lot more expensive than $10,000 in loans offered through the Federal Student Aid Program. Private loans especially are best to be avoided altogether, but with the rising cost of college and the limits on federal aid, many students find that taking out private loans is unavoidable. This is not true: you can avoid taking out private loans.

Keep in mind that if you see private loans listed in your award letter, it is because you have unmet need that the college is assuming you will pay for via private loans. You should realize that you don't have to pay for this shortfall via private loans. You can get the funds through other means including from family or friends (if they can afford anything beyond the EFC), from a PLUS loan, and through outside scholarships, as well as through some other methods we will talk about in some of the coming sections.

Through the rest of this guide, we will be discussing strategies that will help you minimize (or eliminate) your need for private student loans and in some cases all loans completely.

Comparing Award Letters

As you review your award letter, you will want to make sure that you understand it completely. Each school will have their own format for displaying the relevant information, and for this reason, it can sometimes be difficult to compare one school to another.

Award letters are not highly regulated, and you should double check each letter for the following:

Room and Board

Make sure that room and board are included in the estimated cost of attendance. Some colleges will leave this out which will make the full college experience look less expensive than it actually is.

Books and Supplies

Books and supplies are a reality of college, and while the

cost is not directly reflected in the tuition, they still account for money you actually need to pay. Many colleges will include a line item for books and supplies (and sometimes even travel to and from school) in the package, but some schools will not. If this item is missing from your aid letter, make sure you add these expenses to your expected family contribution before comparing the package to another school's award.

Interest Rates on Loans and Years to Repay

Different interests rates can mean the difference of thousands of dollars even if the initial loan balance is the same. You are not required to take out loans from any provider recommended or listed in your award package, but many students do go with the lenders their colleges recommend. Before you sign anything, make sure to look carefully at the interest rate and payment perms (including the number of years to repay the loan and your ability to change the loan payment plan).

In-School Deferment

Make sure you also ask about the possibility of in-school deferment for each of the loans being offered. You will want to know whether or not you will need to pay off your loans while you are in graduate school after college or if you will have to make monthly payments while not making any income. These policies vary from loan to loan.

Front-Loading Grants

A common practice at colleges is to lure new students by

offering them generous financial aid packages the first year of college and then dropping grants and aid in subsequent years. Some schools are more notorious than others (see Chapter 15), but you will definitely want to ask each college about their average aid amount for second year students and beyond versus first-year students to get a sense if you should anticipate a declining package and the approximate amount of aid you can anticipate receiving in future years.

Key Points

- Grants and scholarships are the best form of aid.
- Loans are the least desirable form of aid.
- Unmet need is often hidden in the form of PLUS loans and private loans.
- If loans are a necessity, federal loans are preferable to private loans.
- Be careful when comparing financial aid packages - some are more thorough than others.
- Talk to someone in the financial aid office if any part of your award package is unclear.

Chapter 3
Merit-Based vs Need-Based Aid

Now that we've covered how to apply for aid and how to understand your aid package, we're going to take a step back and talk about aid more generally. There are two different philosophies surrounding aid that dramatically affect the way aid is administered: need-based and merit-based. Each college must choose to allocate its limited financial resources to students, and they must decide if all money is allocated towards need-based aid, all towards merit-based aid, or how they will split their resources to support students based on need in some cases and merit in others.

<u>Need-Based Aid</u>

The first philosophy is the need-based philosophy. This is what we've been talking about so far in the previous two sections. The US government has a need-based philosophy when they administer your aid through the Federal Student Aid Program. On your FAFSA, they ask about your family's income and assets. They don't ask for your grades and test scores. They believe that the amount of aid you receive should be based on how much you are able to afford not based on how academically qualified you are to attend a particular school. Your academic accomplishments are irrelevant to the government as long as you have gained acceptance to an accredited institution and don't fail out. If you can meet that basic benchmark, a mediocre student and an honor role student are exactly the same in the government's eyes.

No matter where you go to college in this country (provided you attend an accredited institution), you will be eligible for need-based aid from the federal government.

In addition to the need-based aid you get through the government, some schools will offer you need-based aid through its own sources. By taking a look at the Expected Family Contribution (EFC) as determined by your FAFSA, the college will subtract this number from the total cost of attendance to determine your financial need. They will then slap on the grants, work-study, and loans you are eligible through the Federal Student Aid Program.

For example, let's say your EFC is $20,000. Let's say the estimated cost of attendance at a college is $60,000 (the cost of attendance should include the full tuition, fees, room, board, books, supplies, and transportation).

A college would look at these numbers and determine that your need is $40,000. With this number in hand, they would then see how much aid you were eligible for through the Federal Student Aid Program. For example, they could see you were eligible for:

Federal Work-Study: $2,500
Stafford Loan: $3,500
Federal Perkins Loan: $2,000

Now, they would add up these numbers and see that $8,000 of the $40,000 of need has been covered, leaving you with a remaining need of $32,000.

At this point, a school's institutional philosophy and financial means matters a lot. Some schools are going to say too bad that you need $32,000. They'll put you in touch with private lenders to help you cover the shortfall or recommend that your parents look into taking out some additional funds through a PLUS loan. Or they'll tell you to apply for outside scholarships.

Many schools, however, will have a need-based financial aid program. They will recognize that you still have significant need and will try to meet it by offering you an institutional grant, money the college gives you as a gift because of need.

Some schools are committed to meeting 100% of demonstrated need (see the "Select Schools That Meet 100% of Need" section), and this may mean that they will offer you a grant equal to the full amount of your remaining need, $32,000. This is an ideal situation since it means that the college is giving you $32,000 in essentially free money you don't have to pay back. With a grant like this, there is no need to take out any private loans, and your public loans are capped at the amount administered through the Federal Student Aid Program, which you can work to reduce through getting outside scholarships as well as some of the other strategies we will talk about later in this book.

Unfortunately, most schools are not going to meet 100% of need even schools that focus their aid strategies on need-based aid, just because of limited resources. In general, wealthier private colleges (which in most cases have a highly competitive admissions process) give the best need-based aid. This is great for the students who can get into these schools, but these colleges are not an option for everyone, and other colleges, despite their best efforts of meeting student need, can not offer grants that cover the majority of student need. You will find that many schools will try to address your need by meeting you somewhere in the middle, offering you a $16,000 institutional grant, for example, and asking you to find the additional $16,000 elsewhere (i.e. have your parents tap into their retirement accounts or take out PLUS loans or have you take out private loans, etc.).

Merit-Based Aid

Merit-based aid is a broad category that includes scholarships offered directly through colleges as well as outside scholarships through independent organizations (including companies, non-profits, and foundations). We are going to talk about outside scholarships in another section, but right now, we will focus on institutional merit-based aid (also known as institutional scholarships).

Just to recap: every college has a limited amount of money they can devote to student aid. What they decide to do with that money is up to their institutional philosophy. Some schools put all of that money into their need-based financial aid programs so that they can offer generous need-based institutional grants which meet close to all of students' demonstrated need. Other schools prefer to set a substantial portion of their financial aid dollars aside for merit-based awards. These colleges may not offer many need-based grants beyond what is offered through the Federal Student Aid Program, but they still may have significant funds available for students with particular interests, talents, or potential. In the example above, we said that you had $32,000 in need after applying funds awarded through the Federal Student Aid Program. We said that if you applied to a school with significant aid funds and a need-based aid philosophy, you might be able to get a $32,000 grant from the school that would cover your full need. But now let's say that you decide to apply to a school that puts all of their aid money into merit aid. In this case, there would be no grants offered to help you cover that $32,000. However, if you have a special talent that the college values such as being an outstanding athlete or artist or community leader, you might be able to get a merit-based scholarship equivalent to $20,000 annually (or whatever the college offers), and you could still effectively reduce your unmet need significantly (or in some cases completely).

Of course, if you were extremely talented and were able to secure a $50,000 per year scholarship because you were not only a highly desirable athlete but also an outstanding student, you might be able to not only eliminate the $32,000, but you could also end up eliminating your federal loans, work-study obligations, and even reduce your family contribution by $10,000. In this scenario, you come out even better than by choosing the school where your $32,000 was covered by need-based aid. But remember that only so many students can get generous merit aid. There isn't enough to go around for everyone so at schools that devote most of their aid to merit-based programs, mediocre students with high need

33

can be left with outrageous loan amounts while the extraordinarily talented students (regardless of their financial situation) get a free or significantly discounted education.

Luckily, there are many different types of merit aid available. Some scholarships award aid to students who have outstanding academic records that exceed the profile of the average student at their school. Colleges might assess academic prowess by looking at grades, test scores, and/or reading the responses to essay questions. In some cases, colleges administer exams and even academic interviews in order to determine the recipients of merit-based aid based on academic credentials. What you need to do to get academically-based merit aid depends on the school and the particular scholarships.

Colleges may also want students based on their extracurricular accomplishments including their skill in a particular sports, their artistic ability, or demonstrated leadership ability.

Other merit-based scholarships are designed to attract students to a school with a particular background, focusing on attracting students from particular geographic regions, first generation college students, children of veterans, or students of a particular cultural or ethnic background.

Some schools may only offer one of these types of scholarships, putting all their aid dollars into academic scholarships, for example, and other schools will spread the funds out among different types of merit-based programs.

The amount of merit-based awards can vary greatly. Some cover only a couple of hundred dollars per semester, and others may cover up to full tuition including fees, room, board, books, supplies, and transportation. Some even provide funding for study abroad experiences, internships, and research opportunities.

The process for applying for merit-based aid varies from school to school and scholarship to scholarship. Some schools will automatically consider you for merit-based options when you submit your application. When I was applying to college, I opened my acceptance letter to Tulane University only to find a letter saying that I had been awarded a $30,000 per year academic scholarship without me even applying. There is no better feeling than getting a surprise merit-based scholarship without having to do any extra work.

That said, quite a few of the best scholarships will require you to submit a separate application. Many of these scholarships will require you to submit an essay (or several) specifically for the scholarship (this is separate from your college application essay). In some cases, you will also be required to submit recommendations and/or have an interview. For art scholarships, you may be asked to submit a portfolio or complete an audition. Oftentimes, the deadlines to do all of these things are early, even before your regular application is due. If you are interested in receiving merit-based aid, you need to start early. Figuring out where you are going to apply by October of your senior year is recommended as many of the deadlines for merit aid are in November and early December.

Which is Better - Need-Based or Merit-Based?

One thing to keep in mind is that whether or not a college focuses its aid packages on merit-based aid or need-based aid, does not reflect the generosity of the school. In terms of aid dollars awarded, there are many colleges that do not offer any merit aid that end up offering more aid than schools with lots of merit-based programs. There are also many schools offering merit aid that offer more than schools that only offer need-based aid.

The way that colleges allocate aid is a merely a system for allocating money; it does not reflect the amount of money distributed.

That said, thinking about how a school allocates their money may be an important part of your search. If you are a student with high need but mediocre credentials, you may be better off at institutions that focus all or most of their aid dollars on need-based aid.

In contrast, if your parents have a high income and you have stellar academic or extracurricular credentials, you may end up getting more money through a merit-based program. In the next section, we'll talk about how to find the best strategies for you.

Key Points

• Apply to schools where you are overqualified in order to maximize merit-based aid (i.e. look for schools where your SAT score and GPA are close to or above the

75th percentile for admitted students).

• Not all colleges will be able to meet your full need (see Chapter 17 for a list of schools that will make this commitment).

• Some students will benefit more from schools that focus on need-based aid while other students will be better served looking at schools that put significant dollars into merit aid (see the Finding the "Best Money-Saving Strategy for You" section).

Strategies

Chapter 4
Finding the Best Money-Saving Strategy For You

In the next two sections of this guide, we are going to cover strategies that can help you save money, and we are going to look at lists of schools that are particularly generous when it comes to distributing financial aid dollars. If you are committed to graduating from college without debt, you will need to figure out how to use these strategies to develop a plan that will allow you to meet your goal. Depending on your circumstances, different strategies might work better than others.

I recommend you read straight through all of the strategies in this section to get a sense of how each strategy can play a part in your college plan, but below I have included a shortcut which will give you an overview of which strategies will likely work best for you (and which resources are most pertinent) based on your academic performance and income level.

<u>Top Academic Performer</u>

You are a top academic performer if you have a 3.8-4.0 GPA unweighted; at least a 1400-1600 SAT (CR+M)/ 31-36 ACT; and have had significant extracurricular involvement including positions of leadership and regional/state/national awards.

Strategy

As a top academic performer, you are likely going to be able to find a way to graduate with little or no debt. You have the highest chances of being admitted to a highly competitive college. Highly competitive colleges are often the most generous colleges when it comes to giving need-based financial aid. You should check out the list of schools committed to meeting 100% of demonstrated need in Chapter 18 . Plus, you may even be able to gain admission to a no loan school (Chapter 17) where you won't have any loans included in your aid package. Even with a generous aid package, you may still decide to reduce your financial burden by applying for outside scholarships (Chapter 8). Another approach as a top academic performer, (and an especially good one for someone who may not qualify for need-based aid), is to look for institutional merit-based scholarships at colleges where you exceed the minimum qualifications. Your in-state colleges will likely provide near full tuition scholarships for top performers and a number of public and private colleges around the country also offer generous scholarships to exceptional students (see Chapter 24 for a list of full tuition scholarships and Chapter 25 for scholarships for National Merit Semifinalist or Finalists). As a top performer, you have the most choice when it comes to graduating from college with no debt. You can take the approach of applying to the most competitive colleges primarily focusing your efforts on getting generous need-based aid or you can look for merit-based programs at schools where you exceed the minimum qualifications. You have ample opportunity to receive outside scholarships as well meaning that whatever path you choose, there is money available to you.

Special Skill or Talent

You qualify as a student with a special skill or talent if you have demonstrated achievement in one of your extracurricular activities that has garnered you significant recognition (usually at the state, national, or international level).

Strategy

If you have a special skill or talent either in the arts, sports, community service, business, or something else, you also have a number of options when it comes to graduating from college with little or no debt. Depending on the strength of your accomplishments, your talent may distinguish you enough in the applicant pool to gain admission to one of the nation's most selective colleges including colleges committed to meeting 100% of demonstrated need (Chapter 18) and which will guarantee you won't have any loans included in your aid package. Most of these most selective colleges will still require that your academic accomplishments are not dramatically out of line with their standards, but depending on the strength of your special skill or talent, you may be able to have grades or scores slightly lower than their 25th percentile mark (you can usually find this data on a college's website in their "class profile" and it is also published by *US News and World Report*). Another option is to look at colleges that offer merit-based aid on the basis of a particular skill or talent. Many colleges offer sports scholarships for recruited athletes, and scholarships for accomplished visual artists, musicians, actors, and dancers are also common (although many of these scholarships have early deadlines and require an audition and/or portfolio submission). Scholarships for students who have demonstrated significant leadership abilities or for students who have been significantly involved in community service activities (Chapter 29) are also available at many colleges and universities. You should also look at outside scholarships (Chapter 8) for awards given to students with your particular skills or talents.

Low Income/Strong Performance

You fall into this category if your household income is below $60,000; you have a minimum 3.6-4.0 GPA unweighted; you have at least a 1250-1600 SAT (CR+M)/ 28-36 ACT; and you've been significantly involved in extracurricular activities.

Strategy

As a low income student with a strong academic performance, your best approach may be to look at the colleges that give away the most generous need-based aid (also frequently the most competitive colleges). You should especially take a look at colleges that meet full need (Chapter 18) or close to it and colleges that do not include loans (Chapter 17) in their aid packages. You are an ideal candidate for many outside scholarships (Chapter 8) many of which take financial aid into account (the Jack Kent Cooke Foundation Scholarship, Elks Most Valuable Student Scholarship, Ronald McDonald House Scholarship, and Gates Millennium Scholarships, and many of the other outside scholarships listed in the resources section of this guide. You also may be qualified to receive significant merit-based scholarships at your in-state public universities or at private universities for which your academic credentials exceed the average applicant. Also make sure to check out the full tuition scholarships (Chapter 24) to see if there are full tuition scholarships you may qualify for.

Other strategies you may want to consider to help you reduce or eliminate your debt load are to consider taking a gap year (Chapter 9) and getting college credit before college (Chapter 10) from AP or IB coursework or classes at your local community college that you took during high school.

Low Income/Mediocre Performance

You fall into this category if your household income is below $60,000; your GPA is at least 2.0-3.5 unweighted; you have a 900-1250 SAT (CR+M)/19-27 ACT; and you've been moderately involved in extracurricular activities.

Strategy

If you are committed to graduating from college with little or no debt, you may need to get creative. Taking a gap year (Chapter 9) can be an excellent way to build yourself a small college fund, and earning a few credits (Chapter 10) at your local community college during high school or while taking a gap year may reduce the number of more expensive credits you are required to take once you enter a four-year school. During your time off, you should consider applying for some outside scholarships (Chapter 8), many of which do not require outstanding academic achievement and are based off a single essay, a project, or competition. College selection will also have an impact on your debt load. Public colleges in your state will offer some of the lowest tuition rates (Chapter 21), and depending on where you live and what you want to study you may also qualify for an out-of-state tuition waiver at schools in neighboring states (Chapter 23) which could reduce your college costs significantly. Tuition guarantee colleges (Chapter 19) are worth considering because they make financial planning easier and free colleges may also be a possibility. Not all free colleges (Chapter 20) require outstanding academic accomplishments, and many preference students with higher need in their admissions process. While in college, taking an internship (Chapter 12) may help you earn money over the summer and could help you later to secure a higher paying job post-graduation that will help you repay any debt immediately.

Medium Income/Strong Performance

You fall into this category if your household income is $60,000-$130,000; you have a 3.6-4.0 GPA unweighted; a 1250-1600 SAT (CR+M)/28-36 ACT; and significant involvement in extracurricular activities.

Strategy

Many people say that middle income students have the toughest time getting money for college, but if you have a strong academic performance, you have many options when it comes to reducing or eliminating your debt load.

Some of most competitive colleges are committed to eliminating student loans (Chapter 17) from all of their aid packages and others may include some federal loans but keep the debt load restricted by being committed to meeting 100% of demonstrated need (Chapter 18). If you decide to attend one of these schools, you may be able to get additional supplemental funds through outside scholarships (Chapter 8). Public universities, especially in-state schools, are also a good option. Your strong performance will likely make you eligible for significant merit-based scholarships that will cover some or all of your tuition at some of the public colleges in your state. You may want to check out states where you can get an out-of-state tuition waiver which will allow you to pay in-state tuition at public colleges in other states (Chapters 22 and 23). Institutional merit-based aid at public and private colleges alike are also worth checking out. You should check the merit-based offerings at every school on your list and make sure to start early because many merit scholarship deadlines come early in November or early December of your senior year (you can also check out the full tuition scholarships in Chapter 24 for some great institutional options). And after you assemble all of your outside aid, institutional merit-based aid, and need-based aid together, if you still need more funds to cover your expenses, see if your college will accept college-level credit earned in high school through AP or IB classes. You may be able to graduate early or reduce your required college credits (Chapter 10) which can mean additional cost savings. If you are still coming up short, consider taking a gap year (Chapter 9) before freshman year which can be a great experience and potentially help you pocket up to $30,000.

Medium Income/Mediocre Performance

You fall into this category if your household income is $60,000-$130,000; you have a GPA 2.0-3.5 unweighted; a 900-1250 SAT (CR+M)/19-27 ACT; and some involvement in extracurricular activities.

Strategy

Oftentimes middle income students with average grades are told that they will have the toughest time getting money for college, but if you are willing to put in the effort, there are still many ways that you can graduate with little or no debt. An obvious solution is to look for colleges with lower tuition rates to begin with. Public colleges in your state are a great option (check out the best deals in your state in Chapter 21) as are colleges where you might be eligible for in-state tuition even if you live out of state because of a regional agreement (Chapter 22). You may also want to consider some of the free colleges (Chapter 20) some of which are not all particularly competitive from an admissions perspective but that can offer a great education for free (often in exchange for a minimum commitment to work a certain number of hours per week). Taking a gap year (Chapter 9) can also be a great way to save money by working a job while living at home with your parents for free. The time off will also allow you to apply for outside scholarships, many of which will not require outstanding grades or extracurricular achievements but are based on single essays, projects, or competition. You may also take a class or two on the side during a year off at your local community college which can help you reduce your required credits and save you money once you arrive at school (Chapter 10).

High Income/Strong Performance

You fall into this category if your household income is above \$130,000; you have a 3.6-4.0 GPA unweighted; a 1250-1600 SAT (CR+M)/28-36 ACT; and significant involvement in extracurricular activities.

Strategy

You might wonder why I'd include high income students in a book about graduating without debt since theoretically high income students should be able to pay for college without taking out loans. Yet college has become so expensive that even many high income families are resorting to loans. Even if they theoretically could afford tuition, paying full tuition may mean sacrificing other things like the tuition at their other kids' private schools, the money they put into their retirement funds, etc. We all have different lifestyles and priorities so even when the FAFSA comes back with an EFC that exceeds the cost of tuition, many families believe that number is unrealistic given their situation and seek other ways to find money for college. The good news is that there are ways to get money even in this situation.

As a high income student looking for college money, your strategy will be significantly different than students with lower or middle incomes. Although you may be surprised to find that even high incomes can sometimes qualify for a small amount of need-based aid at the most generous need-based colleges (Chapter 18) if you describe your particular circumstances to the financial aid department, even at these schools, it is unlikely that you will receive enough need-based to cover any substantial part of your tuition since the college will calculate that you can afford the tuition. If you are committed to going to one of these schools regardless and want to find additional funds to pay for it, you still have options. High income students in many ways benefit the most from outside scholarships since 100% of the funds you earn from a scholarship will directly reduce the amount of money your family needs to contribute to your education (it is counterintuitive, but students with need-based aid packages often will have their aid packages reduced when they get outside aid, lessening the value of any award). Therefore, putting significant effort into finding and applying to outside scholarships can be a very worthwhile endeavor for high income students. As a high-achieving student, you should have a number of options when it comes to receiving outside scholarships (Chapter 8), and you should check out the outside scholarship offerings listed in Chapter 26 and 27 as a place to start and then continue your search by searching the databases for the websites listed in Chapter 30 to help you find additional options. Of course, if you are more flexible about where you might want to go to school or if you do not want to spend your time applying for lots of outside scholarships, you may want to consider colleges that offer merit-based aid to begin with. Not all colleges offer merit-based aid (many of the most competitive colleges don't offer any merit aid or offer very little merit aid) but public colleges and colleges for which you might be slightly more academically qualified than the average admitted student (i.e. your grades and scores are near or above the 75th percentile) could be ideal places to look. You should definitely check out the merit-based opportunities at public colleges in your state, see if you qualify for any tuition waivers (Chapter 23) based on your grades and test scores at public schools in other states and check out the full tuition scholarships in Chapter 24 which may help you find generous institutional scholarships you may be eligible for based on your grades, scores, and achievements. And wherever you go, make sure to ask colleges whether you can use your AP and IB credits (Chapter 10) to graduate early or reduce the number of credits you need to take in order to graduate which can be a great way to reduce the overall cost of college without any additional effort.

High Income/Mediocre Performance

You fall into this category if your household income is above $130,000; you have a GPA 2.0-3.5 unweighted; a 900-1250 SAT (CR+M)/19-27 ACT; and some involvement in extracurricular activities.

Strategy

If you and your family are looking to reduce the cost of college, your best strategy is to focus your efforts on outside scholarships. As a high income student, you will not be eligible for much in the way of need-based aid. And depending on your academic performance and special skills/talents, your choices when it comes to merit-based aid may also be restricted. You may be able to find some merit-based aid a second or third tier schools even with mediocre grades and scores (I especially recommend checking out satellite branches of schools in your state or a smaller regional colleges in your area), but with enough effort you will most certainly be able to get some money via outside scholarships (Chapter 8). There are thousands of outside scholarships available, and many of them are not contingent on your past academic performance. If you write a winning essay, submit a winning art project, or place in a competition, you can get money, and as a high income student without a need-based aid package, every dollar of that money will reduce the amount your family has to pay for your education. If you are really committed to getting the most out of outside scholarships, you may want to consider taking a gap year. You can work a job to earn additional money for college, get an internship (Chapter 12) or earn college credits (Chapter 10) at your local community college which can also save you money down the line. At the same time, you'll have a year extra to accumulate cash by applying to outside scholarships without the burden of being in school and applying to college at the same time giving you a significant advantage to high school seniors who have limited time to write additional essays and search for scholarships.

If the idea of applying for lots of outside scholarships doesn't appeal, the easiest way to save money on your tuition is to pick a less expensive college in the first place. Check out the public colleges in your state (you can find the best in-state deals in Chapter 21) and schools with regional agreements (Chapter 22) that will reduce the typical out-of-state costs at public colleges in neighboring states. Choosing colleges with tuition guarantees (Chapter 19) will also help you plan out your finances and looking at some colleges where at least 25% of students who do not have need-based aid receive merit-based aid (meaning merit aid qualifications are not significantly higher than admissions qualifications) may also be a good strategy (Chapter 16).

Low Performance

You fall into this category if your GPA is less than a 2.0; you have below 900 on the SAT (CR+M)/under 19 ACT; and minimal or no extracurricular activities.

Strategy

As a low performer who is motivated to go to college, you can still find money from a variety of sources including from outside scholarships based on a single essay, project, or competition (Chapter 8). More than anyone, however, you may benefit from spending the first year or two out of college attending your local community college where you can earn college credits you can later apply to a four-year college (Chapter 10). The tuition there will likely be significantly lower than even at your lowest cost in-state four-year college, and you'll save money by being able to live at home while in school. Plus, if you can earn strong grades during your time there, you may eligible for merit-based institutional grants (many public colleges offer awards specifically for transfer students so this is something to look into). You'll end up graduating with a four-year degree having spent less money than if you enrolled straight out of college and having graduated perhaps from a school with a better reputation.

Key Points

- Your strategy for getting aid will depend on your income level and performance.
- Students with high income are less likely to benefit from need-based aid.

- Students with low income can get generous scholarships from schools that have a strong need-based aid program.
- Top performers have many options when it comes to aid. They are the most likely to receive merit-based aid, but if they choose to attend a school with limited merit-based options can still likely get additional funds from outside scholarships (and from need-based programs if they qualify).
- Students with mediocre grades and scores can use the methods discussed in the following chapters such as taking a gap year, studying abroad, earning college credit before college, and getting internships to save money in college. They also may qualify for some less conventional outside scholarships which evaluate students on the basis of one essay, a project, or activity.

Chapter 5
Identify the Right Public Colleges

All colleges are expensive, but often at half the price (or even less) of their private counterparts, public colleges are a good place to start if you are looking to save money. Although the numbers vary significantly state by state and school by school, the average cost of tuition and fees in 2013-2014 at public colleges was $8,893 for in-state residents and $22,203 for out-of-state residents. In contrast, the average cost of tuition and fees at private colleges was $30,094 with tuition at many of the most exclusive private colleges close to $50,000 not including room and board.

While comparing the prices of public and private colleges based on sticker price alone is not always a fair comparison (because private colleges are also usually the most generous when it comes to financial aid meaning that the actual cost of tuition may very well be equivalent or less than at public colleges), public colleges are definitely worthy of consideration for any student looking to save money.

In-State Tuition

When you choose a public college in the state where you currently reside, you are guaranteed to get the in-state tuition rate which can save you up to $100,000 over the course of four years when compared to the most expensive private options (see the Chapter 21 for a list of the best in-state deals in each state). Furthermore, there is a good chance you may qualify for one of the many merit-based scholarships offered to in-state students. Scholarships specifically designated for in-state students are particularly appealing due to the limited applicant pool (i.e. they are less competitive to get because only in-state students are eligible to receive them). Many state colleges offer scholarships on the basis of not only academic achievement but also artistic talents, community service, debating skills, leadership experience, and/or sports which means there are multiple opportunities to receive supplementary money.

State colleges tend to be more diverse in terms of the quality of the student body than at many private schools. Although a state may have one or two flagship universities that are highly competitive, most schools have significantly less competitive branches as well that attract a wide range of students. Even as a student with a B or even C average, you may be above average academically for students entering into some of the satellite campuses. Because these satellite branches are eager to recruit high performing students, they are often great places to find easily accessible academic scholarships ranging from a few hundred dollars per year all the way to full tuition.

Because these institutions are state run, you will need to do your research on your particular state to find out more about which satellite campuses offer the best scholarship options and which ones would be the best match for you based on your academic performance. That said, if you do your research, the payoff for getting a scholarship at a public in-state university is huge - there is a good chance you will be able to graduate with very minimal debt, if any, regardless of your family's income and even if you are only an average student.

Out-of-State Tuition

Even if you are interested in attending a public college in another state, there are still likely to be significant financial benefits. Although tuition is higher for out-of-state students than in-state students, out-of-state tuition in most cases is still considerably less than at most private universities. Plus these days, many public universities offer merit-based scholarship opportunities for out-of-state students as well which can cover up to full tuition.

Of course, most students would want to get the in-state base tuition rate if it was available, and although this is not possible most of the time, there are some instances in which out-of-state students are eligible for the lower in-state cost. For students who have parents in the military or who have a parent who is a policeman or fireman and who reside out of state, you can sometimes get your residency requirement waived. Alternatively, if you grew up right on the state line and wish to attend the public college right across the border, you can in some parts of the country petition to be able to pay the in-state rate.

Some colleges, such as Texas A&M University, will automatically offer the in-state tuition rate to any student who receives a merit-based scholarship valued at $1,000 or more. Similarly, the University of Arkansas waives some of the fees for out-of-state students for some of its scholarship winners (for a more complete list of colleges that offer out-of-state fee waivers based on achievement, see Chapter 23). Depending on the region of the country you are in, you also may be eligible for regional exchange partnerships which allow you to attend a school in a neighboring state at a discounted out-of-state price (see Chapter 22).

Of course some students try to go for the more obvious approach; establishing residency in a new state. If you are under the age of 23, this is a tricky process. The government considers you to be a resident of wherever your parents live (and pay taxes) unless you petition a school to consider you an independent. Becoming an independent is often a long and tedious process, has a low success rate, and in the event of success will cause additional financial obstacles like covering your own health insurance since you will no longer be able to rely on your family's plan. The most successful cases of getting independent status typically involve homeless students, students over the age of 24, married students, and students with a child.

Even as an independent, most colleges will require that you live in a state for at least a year before beginning school. You will need to prove that you moved to the state for reasons beyond trying to get in-state tuition. Spending a year working and paying taxes and registering your car in the new state will substantially increase your odds of success. Still, trying to establish residency is a risky and time-consuming process and best used as a last resort.

Public Colleges for Top Performers

As a top performer academically, state schools can be

phenomenal options from a financial perspective. If your academic credentials put you closer to the 75th percentile or higher, there is a good chance you will be eligible for one of the many half tuition or full tuition scholarships available for top in-state students in most states. Some of these scholarships are automatic, meaning that if you have a certain GPA and SAT score, you are guaranteed to get the scholarship assuming you gain admission to the university.

While all of this sounds great financially, as a top student, you may hesitate choosing a state school over a top-rated private college where you'd also likely be able to gain admission. This is a valid concern and definitely a decision you need to make for yourself. There are significant differences between the experiences of going to a private university over a public one. In general, for example, private universities are smaller than public universities. They tend to be less bureaucratic, have smaller average class sizes, and often offer a stronger name brand. These are valid and legitimate differences that are worthy of consideration. Still, dismissing public colleges altogether would be a mistake. Besides the aforementioned financial benefits, being a top student at a public university may provide you with other benefits as well. Many public universities now offer honors colleges which are exclusive communities within the larger university community that offer you access to small seminar-style classes with the top professors, priority in course registration, guaranteed on-campus housing, and other benefits. Choosing an honors college at a public university may allow you to create something equivalent to a private university experience at a significantly discounted rate.

- Attending an in-state institution is a good way to save money.
- Besides the fact that their sticker price is often lower to begin with, public colleges typically offer significant merit-based aid specifically for in-state residents on the basis of academics, artistic talents, and/or sports. Even out-of-state residents with outstanding achievements are often offered merit-based aid.
- You can get in-state tuition rates at schools in neighboring states through regional tuition agreements or through merit-based scholarships that will allow exceptional out-of-state students to pay in-state fees.
- Top performers can often get generous merit-based scholarships at public colleges (both in their states and elsewhere) that will cover between half and full tuition (and sometimes include fees, room, board, and stipends for books and summer activities).
- Honors colleges can give top students a similar academic experience as a private liberal arts college within a public university.

Potential Savings

- Up to $100,000 in tuition savings over four years.
- Up to $40,000 if you decide to live at home and commute to school.

Chapter 6
Don't Forget Private Options

There are many reasons why students choose to attend private colleges including their on average smaller size, less bureaucratic policies, and more cohesive campus cultures. Students at private colleges and universities on average graduate in less time, have smaller class sizes, and less volatility due to the political climates (since public universities are often dependent on some state funding).

And yet many students do not even consider private colleges because of their on average higher price tags. It is understandable that many students shy away from any private college when they see published tuition rates of over $40,000 (the average tuition at a private university today include room and board) or even over $60,000 at the most selective colleges. But although private colleges on average have more expensive sticker prices, private colleges also tend to be the most generous when it comes to distributing financial aid. In fact, 90% of students at private colleges receive some sort of financial aid, and with the average aid package valued at $22,000 per student, many of these packages were significant. It surprises many people to learn that private colleges often equally diverse student bodies as public colleges and universities.

Because private colleges are given significant latitude in determining their philosophies of distributing aid, it can be very difficult to understand the true cost of attending any given college until you apply and see what you are awarded. Each school has their own system of distributing aid, and at many schools, there are students paying the full price as well as students paying nothing at all (and many in between).

As a prospective student, a number far more important to consider than the sticker price is the expected net price of your education. The net price is the published tuition minus the scholarship and grant money that you receive.

Net Price = Published Tuition - Scholarship and Grant Money

Because the net price is largely dependent on who you are (in terms of your income for need-based aid and your grades, scores, and extracurricular activities for merit-based awards), it can be difficult to assess when you are trying to figure out where to apply. Many colleges have net price calculators you can use to get an approximation of what sort of grant and scholarship aid you might receive at their school. You can find these calculators on many colleges' websites, but you also may want to check out the College Board's Net Price Calculator (http://studentnpc.collegeboard.org) which allows you to calculate net price easily for a number of participating schools.

It is good to keep in mind that while these calculators can help you anticipated aid at one school versus another, they are only providing you with estimates. The actual aid your receive may be higher or lower, but if you follow some of the other advice in this such as negotiating with the student aid office to increase your grant money and applying for institutional scholarships, it is more likely that your aid package will be close to as generous or even more generous than is initially reflected using a net price calculator.

The key point here is to realize that there are private colleges where the net price of attendance can actually be lower than at public colleges even if the sticker price is significantly higher. Whether this is true for you or not at any particular school depends on your income level and accomplishments. You need to do your research to figure out which private schools will offer you the best deal. But if you put in the time (and I also recommend looking at all the metrics we will talk about in Chapter 7), and if you make an effort to consider some of the schools that have made major commitments to financial aid programs (such as schools that are committed to meeting 100% of need, free colleges, schools with a high percentage of merit aid offered, or schools that offer aid packages with no student loans), you will likely be able to find private college options with comparable or even more favorable pricing plans than at public universities.

Key Points

- Private colleges can be just as affordable (if not more affordable) than public colleges.
- The net price of college is more important than the sticker price.
- Use net price calculators to help determine your expected net price.

Potential Savings

- The difference between one private college's net price and another's can vary by tens of thousands of dollars so doing your research beforehand can save you $40,000-$60,000 over the course of four years.

Chapter 7
Collect Data

Data empowers you. Colleges are not always upfront about how they distribute aid and their financial philosophies. The more information you can get about a college before finalizing your college list, the better off you are.

The key here is to do your research upfront. The sooner you start, the more time you will have to gather information and refine your college list accordingly.

I recommend starting by finding the percentage of students who receive aid at each school you are considering. Another figure to check is the average aid package. You can find this information free online by searching for each of the schools on your list on CollegeData (http://www.collegedata.com)

Once you have a sense of a school's financial aid program, you also will want to do more in-depth research about the school's financial aid philosophy. Here are some good questions to answer:

• Is the school committed to meeting 100% of demonstrated need? If not, what percentage of need does it meet?
• Does the school guarantee full tuition need-based

scholarships to students whose parents earn below a certain threshold of income?

- Does the school include loans in their financial aid package or is their a cap on the amount of loans they will include in the package?
- How much money do they give away in merit scholarships?
- What are the scholarship opportunities and are they renewable annually?
- Do the merit-based scholarships have separate applications, and if so, when are the deadlines?
- Are there any automatic scholarships based on having a certain GPA or test score?
- How does the school modify your need-based aid package when you earn outside scholarships (i.e do they reduce your self-help first like loans and work-study or do they eliminate institutional grants)?

Other pertinent information may include:

- The percentage of students who graduate within four years (since taking longer to graduate means spending more money).
- The average rate of tuition increase over the past couple of years.
- The cost of living in off-campus housing close to the campus and whether or not students are allowed to live off-campus.

If you can't find this information on the website of each school on your list, email the financial aid office directly. Not only will they be able to provide you with answers, but by showing an active interest in the school, you will increase the odds of building a relationship with the people who are going to be determining your aid package (which can be a scarily subjective process especially at a private university), and your effort may positively affect the package you are offered.

Key Points

• Although the sticker price at private colleges is often high, most students usually pay much less.

• Every college has its own methodology for granting aid - some schools only offer need-based aid, some merit-based aid, and others offer a combination of the two. The breakdown of the aid packages in terms of institutional grants, loans, and work study components often vary school to school.

• Some colleges will award merit-based aid based on your general application for admission while others have a separate application process for each scholarship they offer.

• Many private colleges give away full tuition scholarships (see Chapter 24 for some examples).

Potential Savings

• Varies significantly but in some cases can be the difference to getting a full ride scholarship at one school versus paying the sticker price at another (a total of up to $250,000 in savings).

Chapter 8
Apply for Outside Scholarships

You've probably heard about essay contests or awards from local clubs and companies that will get you money for college. There are thousands of scholarships offering money for college administered by independent organizations which you can use at any school to which you apply. In theory, these sound like a great way to earn money for college because they are so flexible. But outside scholarships have some serious limitations, and while they certainly do have a place for any student hoping to graduate from college without any debt, they should not be the end all and be all of your college financing strategy.

Many people are surprised to learn that outside scholarships, or scholarships not directly affiliated with a particular institution, only account for approximately 5% of the financial aid available for American college students. The majority of aid comes from state and federal funds as well as directly from colleges. The award amount of each outside scholarship varies. Many local scholarships may only be for a few hundred dollars. Some national scholarships can cover close to your full tuition. In terms of competitiveness, some scholarships are given to everyone who applies who meets a certain set of criteria where others are awarded to fewer than 1% of applicants. Some are based off of academic merits whereas others are based purely on an essay, leadership activity, or specific talent. Some are restricted to or favor students from a particular ethnic background, or for students whose parents work for a particular company, or confined to students from a particular geographic location.

The Federal Overaward Regulation

One of the most important things to understand about outside scholarships before you rush out and start applying is how the money awarded to you will be used. Many students mistakenly believe that every dollar they earn in scholarships is one dollar their family will save. This is not usually true.

The Federal Overaward Regulation states that outside scholarships count as financial resources that will reduce your aid package dollar for dollar. How your aid package is reduced will depend on the policy of each college. For example, let's say that your college has awarded you a financial aid package that consists of the following:

Work-study: $1,500
Student Loans: $5,000
Institutional Grant: $10,000
Parental Contribution: $20,000
Total Cost of Attendance: $36,500

After you receive this offer, you are awarded a $3,000 scholarship. You are required by law to report this award to the college. You are probably hoping that they will reduce the parental contribution from $20,000 to $17,000, but this will not happen. Your scholarship will first reduce the amount of aid you are receiving. Some schools might just reduce the $10,000 grant to a $7,000. This is the most frustrating of all scenarios because it makes all of the effort you put into receiving the scholarship feel worthless. Since a grant is just receiving free money, receiving less free money because you worked hard to get a scholarship is frustrating.

The best scenario is for a college to reduce the student loan portion of your financial aid package or eliminate the work-study (or a combination of the two). Some schools are more than willing to accommodate this request, and in this case would, for example, reduce the $5,000 in student loans down to $2,000. Because student loans ultimately balloon up to much more than the initial loan amount, applying a scholarship to a student loan certainly makes them worthwhile saving you all of the interest you would have incurred had you not received the scholarship.

Whether a school will allow you to apply an outside scholarship to loans or not is up to them. You need to ask each school specifically, and you may find that the schools on your list have vastly different policies. Some will accommodate easily while others will require a 50% split with institutional grants. Some will not allow you to reduce your loan amount at all until you earn enough in outside scholarships to eliminate grants.

If there are three schools that all charge $36,500 in tuition and offer you an initial aid package that looks like the one we just outlined above, all three of these examples reflect how they could readjust your aid package after you received a $3,000 scholarship:

School A - Full Grant Reduction Policy
Work-study: $1,500
Student Loans: $5,000
Institutional Grant: $7,000
Parental Contribution: $20,000
Outside Scholarship: $3,000
Total Cost of Attendance: $36,500

School B - Split Grant Reduction Policy
Work-study: $1,500
Student Loans: $3,500
Institutional Grant: $8,500
Parental Contribution: $20,000
Outside Scholarship: $3,000
Total Cost of Attendance: $36,500

School C - Loan Reduction Policy
Work-study: $1,500
Student Loans: $2,000
Institutional Grant: $10,000
Parental Contribution: $20,000
Outside Scholarship: $3,000
Total Cost of Attendance: $36,500

As you can see from the examples above, School C is the most ideal policy allowing you apply the full $3,000 to your student loans. School A on the other hand is the least ideal policy preventing you from benefitting from your outside scholarship at all. The good news is that most schools will allow you to at least apply some of an outside scholarship to loans or work-study, but many schools will only allow you to upon request. If you don't say anything, there is a good chance your grant amount will become reduced without you even noticing. To prevent this from happening, make sure to ask each school on your list about their specific policy.

Unmet Need

As we just discussed, outside scholarships will generally reduce your aid package by reducing work-study, institutional grants, or loans due to federal law. There is one exception to this system, however, and that is if a college has been unable to meet your full need. Let's say we take the same example from above but change it slightly so that the financial aid package is as follows:

School D - School with Unmet Need
Work-study: $1,500
Student Loans: $5,000
Institutional Grant: $10,000
Parental Contribution: $20,000
Unmet Need: $3,000
Total Cost of Attendance: $39,500

In this example, the numbers are entirely the same except the cost of tuition at the school is higher. The college has offered you a package that was unable to meet your full need. There are still $3,000 in this case unaccounted for. Colleges put this number in the package hoping you can find the funds to cover the shortfall via private loans, PLUS loans, or outside scholarships. If you receive an outside scholarship and you have unmet need, colleges will typically allow you to apply the scholarship to the unmet need portion of the package before reducing other parts of your aid package such as your institutional grants or loans.

Reducing Your Parental Contribution

You can use outside scholarships and/or institutional merit scholarships to reduce the parental contribution if you earn more money through scholarships than the sum total of your need-based financial aid package. This is tough to do especially if you are a student with high need, but it is possible. For example, let's say your financial aid package consists of the following:

Original Financial Aid Award
Student Loans: $5,000
Institutional Grant: $8,000
Parental Contribution: $16,000
Total Cost of Attendance: $29,000

Now let's say you earn a $20,000 scholarship from an outside source. The college will now update your aid package to appear as follows:

Financial Aid Award After $20,000 Outside Scholarship
Student Loans: $0
Institutional Grant: $0
Parental Contribution: $9,000
Outside Scholarship: $20,000
Total Cost of Attendance: $29,000

As you can see above, the first $13,000 of your scholarship was used to wipe out the institutional grant and student loans. But with $20,000 in scholarship, you still have $7,000 left. That extra $7,000 can now be applied to the parental contribution reducing that to $9,000. Of course, receiving outside scholarships this large is hard. There aren't many scholarships that offer that amount of money, but there are some, and when you combine outside scholarships with institutional aid you get through a merit-based program at your school, large cost reductions are possible. Keep in mind, however, that you are only allowed to receive up $300 over the cost of attendance via scholarship. If after adding together outside scholarships with institutional aid your total aid package exceeds $300 of the total cost you will not be able to receive your full aid award. In this scenario, the best thing to do is to speak with the sponsors of your outside scholarship about distributing your scholarship awards in smaller pieces across all four years of college which may prevent this problem and still allow you to reap the full value of your scholarship spread out over several years.

For a list of top paying outside scholarships, see Chapter 26, and for some additional options, look at Chapter 27. You may also want to check out some of the institutional merit-based scholarships we cover in Chapters 24 (full tuition scholarships), Chapter 25 (National Merit Scholarships), Chapter 28 (arts scholarships), and Chapter 29 (community service and leadership scholarships).

Another approach is to apply for many smaller scholarships to total a large sum. This is a tiring and complicated approach that few students have the time and energy to pursue, but it has been a successful strategy for some students who have managed to apply to enough small obscure scholarships to end up putting together aid packages that total $15,000 or more. If you are interested in taking this approach, my recommendation is to start as early as possible. Spend the summer before your senior year applying and the summer after senior year applying for even more. Applying to scholarships is like a part-time job, and the students who are the most successful take it that seriously.

You can find some of the best resources to search for scholarships in Chapter 30.

Scholarships for Students Not Applying for Need-Based Aid

If you are not applying for any need-based aid, the entire value of an outside scholarship or merit scholarship will reduce your out-of-pocket expenses. Thus, if you were planning on paying the full sticker price at your in-state public university of $14,000 and you receive an $8,000 scholarship, you will only need to pay $6,000 meaning each dollar of the scholarship value ends up being a full dollar of out-of-pocket savings.

Benefits of Outside Scholarships

After reading this section, you may feel like applying for outside scholarships isn't as worthwhile as you initially thought. Between finding scholarships for which you will be competitive, writing essays, and only directly benefiting for some of the value of the scholarship at many schools, it may not seem worth the effort. It is important to keep in mind that in addition to being a great financial resource, receiving a scholarship is also an honor that can be used to enhance your application for admission. Furthermore, some schools offer non-monetary awards to recipients of outside scholarships such as priority in the housing lottery or research assistant opportunities. It is worth asking the financial aid office at each college about any non-monetary incentives they have for students to receive outside scholarships.

Key Points

- There are outside scholarships available for every type of student.
- Outside scholarships can award significant amounts of money.
- Outside scholarships will not reduce your expected family contribution until the amount you get in scholarships exceeds your unmet need and need-based aid award.
- Gaining outside scholarships will reduce your need-based aid package once all of your unmet need has been satisfied, but upon request, but you may be able to reduce the loan portion of your package rather than the grant portion making the funds worthwhile (check with each college on your list about their policy of how they allocate funds from outside scholarships).
- Applying for scholarships can be time-consuming and it is recommended that you plan to start early if you are looking to get significant awards.
- Many scholarships are not particularly competitive (especially local scholarships). If you apply for enough, you will likely be able to find money.

Potential Savings

- Getting up to full tuition is possible.
- Top performers often get $3,000-$10,000 if they apply to at least 10 relevant scholarships (and for the

most competitive scholarships can end up winning substantially more).

• Most students can get at least $500-$2,500 with enough effort (and mediocre students who are willing to write enough essays and enter some of the very lucrative essay contests have been able to college $20,000-$40,000).

Chapter 9
Take a Gap Year

More students should take a gap year. There are many benefits to taking some time off between high school and college, and the financial benefits account for only some of them. Students who take time off are more likely to graduate in four years when they do return to college. They tend to be more focused. They tend to change their major fewer times. They graduate on average with higher GPAs. They are also able to accumulate a year's worth of life experience (and in many cases job experience) which can be a tremendous asset.

Taking a year off might seem like a drastic step, but if you are serious about graduating without debt, it might be something to consider. Chances are, if you are just finishing high school, you are still living at home with your parents. You aren't paying for rent, and you aren't paying for food, and for the most part, all of the money you earn is yours to keep. This is a pretty unique situation. Most people in this country have to spend most if not all of their earnings just to live off of. At least right now, you don't have to. If you get a job, even a job that pays close to minimum wage at a local retail store or restaurant, for example, you will actually be able to save a significant amount of money. One year of working full-time can easily add up to $20,000 or $30,000. If you are awarded a scholarship worth that amount, you'd probably be ecstatic. It is a lot of money. By itself, it could pay for two years of college at many in-state universities and at the very least will put a significant dent in reducing your loans at other institutions.

Now imagine that if in addition to working, you spend your evenings and free time applying for outside scholarships. Remember that you are no longer in school. You don't have homework to deal with in the evenings. When you get off of work, you are done. If you make an effort to apply for two scholarships per week for the year, you will have applied to 100 outside scholarships by the end of your year off. Almost no high school students apply for that number of scholarships. Between school, extracurricular activities, and everything else it is just not realistic. An ambitious high school student might get around to doing 5. Applying for 100 is practically unheard of, but if you put effort into each one and choose them well, this can be a winning strategy. Even if you only win 10% of those scholarships, and each scholarship pays an average of $1,000, that is $10,000 in additional money right there. If you get lucky and win one or two big ones, that number might balloon to $25,000 or $35,000 in scholarship money. Add that figure to the earnings from your job, and you can see that you likely won't have to take out any loans when you start college in the fall.

You don't have to be an extraordinary student to make this plan work. Any high school graduate can get some job after graduation, and there are scholarship opportunities even for mediocre students. Many scholarship opportunities evaluate applicants purely on the basis on one essay and others care more about your ethnic background or other affiliations than your grades or test scores. The key is finding scholarships that fit you, and if you have the luxury of time, any student can find a handful of scholarships where they can be competitive.

You might be uninspired by the idea of taking a year of working full-time at a minimum wage job. Having the opportunity to work at a lower-level job can be a phenomenal learning experience, but if you are looking for something a bit more intellectually stimulating, you may have more options than you realize. Ask your friends' parents if their companies might consider hiring a paid intern for a full-time position for the year. Email local businesses related to your interests (e.g. medical offices, law firms, and newspapers) asking if they have any opportunities for an ambitious high school grad taking a year off to earn money and gain experience before going to college. You might think that you have little to offer these sorts of companies, but you might be surprised. If you were a good student with a proven track record of working hard, they may see you as a valuable asset. Because you are young, they don't have to pay you much, and if you present yourself well, they might think you would be a hard worker. You might not get paid much more than you would working at your local mall, but you will gain valuable work experience in one of these jobs if you can make it work. In the best case scenario, you might even get a job offer good after you graduate from college (I knew several people in college who after graduating went on to work for the companies they worked for while taking a gap year), and in any case, the experience will help you get internships during college, improve your resume, and potentially help you secure a high-paying job after college which of course will help you pay off any college loans you might eventually take out.

Key Points

- Taking a gap year is one of the best ways to reduce college costs.
- Your living expenses are minimal if you live at home with your parents and are covered by their health insurance.
- You can earn money by working.
- You can spend your free time applying for outside scholarships, giving you a leg up over many of the high school seniors you are competitive with who are concurrently enrolled in school and very busy.
- You may also take a class or two at the local community college which can help you earn college credit which can save you money later on.

Potential Savings

- Total savings of up to $60,000.
- $20,000-$30,000 from working.
- $10,000-$30,000 (and sometimes more) in outside scholarship money.

Chapter 10
Earn College Credits Before College

These days, most public high schools offer either AP classes, which are designed to be college-level courses. If you take the exam offered at the end of each AP course and get a score of 4 or 5 (and even 3 in some cases), you may be able to gain college credit once you matriculate in college. Credits, in many cases, equal money. If you take four AP courses, for example, you may be able to pass out of an entire semester of college work saving you anywhere from $6,000 to $35,000 once you account for room, board, fees, and other expenses. With seven or eight AP courses, you may be able to graduate an entire year early potentially saving you anywhere from $12,000 to $70,000.

Not every college will allow you to apply your AP credits to college, but many will. Some schools will let you use them for passing out of an introductory course, but will not let you use them for college credit (meaning you won't be able to use them to graduate early) whereas other will give them the exact same weight as any course offered by their institution. You will want to ask the schools you apply to for each of their specific policies.

Of course there are pros and cons to graduating early. From a financial perspective, it is a great way to save money. But presumably you are going college for other reasons too. You probably are looking to have a certain academic and social experience that may feel restricted condensed into three or three-and-a-half years. While some students are comfortable with a condensed schedule, other students want to have the full four-year experience. If you want to graduate with your class but also want to benefit from the cost savings you can get from early graduation, you may consider taking a year off in the middle of your college experience. Many students who do this end up living near school and getting a job or internship. They are able to stay fully integrated in the college community during their time off while participating in an activity that will prepare them for their career and potentially earn them money.

If you spend the job working full-time, even at a job that pays just slightly over minimum wage, you could save $10,000-$30,000 per year. Add that to the savings you accrue by not paying for a fourth year of college, and you can save up to $100,000 when you decide to apply your AP credits to knock a year off of your time in college.

If you were not able to take AP classes in high school, there may be other ways to gain college credit that will allow you to graduate early. Some colleges will accept IB credits instead of AP credits (if your high school offered the International Baccalaureate program). Many colleges will also allow you to apply credits you earned at other college-level institutions such as your local community college. Community college courses which you may have taken while still in high school (many high schools allow you to enroll concurrently in community college classes) or during your summer vacations cost significantly less per credit than at most four-year universities. The foundational course options such as calculus courses and foreign language will likely cover very similar content to what you'd find at any four-year school but be offered at a more reasonable price.

You also may want to consider taking a couple of exams through the College Board's College-Level Examination Program which allows students the opportunity to take an exam to demonstrate mastery of college-level material. Exams are offered in 33 subjects, and for each exam you pass you may be able to earn up to 12 college credits at the 2,900 colleges that accept CLEP exams. You can take the CLEP exams at testing centers located at any of the 1,700 test centers throughout the country, and for $77 per test, they can end up saving you hundreds or even thousands of dollars when compared to the cost of enrolling in a college course.

Key Points

- AP or IB credits will sometimes reduce your required credits for college graduation.
- Courses taken at your local community college (or any accredited college) may also count.
- Taking enough pre-college credits may reduce your tuition at colleges that charge tuition based on number of credits that you are taking each semester.
- If you accumulate enough credits to graduate a semester or a year early, you may be able to save significant amounts of money by not only saving on tuition but also on the room, board, and living expenses associated with being in school.
- If you are able to graduate in fewer than 8 semesters, you could decide to take a semester or year off

85

in the middle of your college experience to work and earn additional money to finance your education and still graduate on-time with your class.

Potential Savings

- $6,000-$35,000 if you can pass out of a semester.
- $12,000-$70,000 if you can pass out of a year.
- Up to $100,000 when you can pass out of two semesters and take this time off in the middle of college to live at home and work.
- Reducing your credit load during any semester can save you $1,000-$15,000 at colleges that bill by credit hour.

Chapter 11
Study Abroad

Many students want to study abroad for reasons entirely unrelated to financial aid including the opportunity to visit a different country, experience a new culture, and learn a language. However, study abroad can in some cases also be an opportunity to save money. This is a complex topic because your ability to save money through study abroad will vary significantly depending on the college you decide to attend.

At some schools, studying abroad will definitely not save you money. Many students, in fact, find the semester they studies abroad to be one the most expensive of their college careers. But at other schools, you might be able to save tons of money by studying abroad. I saved over $10,000 in the one semester I studied abroad based on the study abroad policy at my school. Asking about how your college handles study abroad will help you figure out whether study abroad can help you reduce your overall college expense while providing you with many other benefits as well.

The first thing to understand is that the tuition at American colleges is one of the highest tuition rates in the world. If you enroll in a university in just about any other country, the cost of a semester will likely be only a fraction of what you pay in the United States regardless of whether of you attend a public or private school. Theoretically, being able to gain course credit at another university that charges much less than your home university could be a great way to save money. And sometimes it is. This is exactly what happened to me. My school allowed me to to enroll directly in a Chilean university at the cost of tuition there. I had to pay a small administrative fee to my school (under $1,000) but other than that, I did not have to pay any other fees directly to my college in order to receive credit that semester. And yet, the financial aid package transferred (at least up to the value of the cost of tuition at the Chilean university). Colleges that let you pay only the cost of tuition at the foreign university will likely save you thousands of dollars even after adding the additional expense of travel to and from the country.

Of course, many American universities have realized that study abroad can be a profitable venture for them. Some schools require that you pay the full tuition rate to them in order to receive academic credit even if the actual cost of enrolling in a foreign university is significantly less than at your home university (they end up pocketing the difference and make lots of money). While they may allow your financial aid to transfer, you will still likely be responsible for the same parental contribution as normal plus increased travel expenses. Still, even if your school has adopted this kind of policy, you may still be able to save money when it comes to room and board. Depending on the country where you choose to study, room and board expenses may be significantly lower than at your home university, sometimes strikingly so. In some places, students have been able to save close to $8,000 per year (or $4,000 per semester) amounting to savings that can amount to overall savings even after taking into account the cost of airfare. One other place students have been able to save money is related to textbooks. Many other countries do not have the same culture of asking students to purchase textbooks (they either don't rely on textbooks or include their cost in tuition) which can save you close to $1,000 per semester. In Chile, for example I took four courses and was not asked to purchase any additional supplies for any of these courses.

The worst situation is when you attend a school that will not allow your financial aid to transfer or a school that requires you to pay full tuition fees to your home college as well as program fees for your study abroad program. Usually, you will only find these kind of policies if you are interested in studying abroad via a program not already approved through your school. Thus, it is highly recommended that you do a search on approved study abroad programs prior to selecting a college in order to make sure you can find a satisfactory option so you do not run into this situation.

Overall, studying abroad can be a good way to save money especially if your college allows you to opt out of the regular tuition rate and pay the program cost of the program directly. In some cases, you may be able to save close to $30,000 annually (or $15,000 per semester) if you are able to find an affordable enough study abroad program and after taking into account savings you also accrue from lower room and board expenses.

Even at schools that require you to pay their full tuition rate during study abroad, you may still be able to get $3,000-$6,000 in savings after taking into account lower room and board expenses and book savings.

You should ask about your school's study abroad system before you decide to enroll. Ask them if your financial aid transfers, if there are programs that have typically saved students money, and make sure there are enough approved programs to meet your needs.

Key Points

- Different colleges have different policies when it comes to financing study abroad. At some schools, you will lose money by studying abroad, but at others it can be a source of significant cost savings.
- Ask colleges whether students studying abroad are required to pay regular tuition rates or if they can pay the institutional fee or program fee wherever they plan to study
- Research the room and board rates in program's location.
- Make sure your financial aid package will transfer to your study abroad program and if there will be any modifications.

Potential Savings

- Up to $4,000 per semester (or $8,000 per year) in room and board savings (varies significantly from country to country and program to program).
- Up to $15,000 per semester (or $30,000 per year) when you enroll in a college that allows you to pay fees directly to a foreign university or study abroad program for credit and where living expenses are minimal.

Chapter 12
Do Internships

Students with loans used to be told to spend their summers working a summer job to help pay for college. Thirty years ago, the money you could earn from even a low level summer job such as working as a lifeguard or a camp counselor could cover a substantial portion of your tuition. Now this is no longer the case. Even with the advantages that come with living at home with your parents and not having to pay any rent over the summer, most summer jobs won't end up netting you more than a few thousand dollars by the summer's end. If you choose to take a job in another part of the country in the world, you'll likely end up netting almost nothing (or even end up losing money) after taking into account room, board, and transportation expenses.

Earning any money can certainly be a help, but I would recommend you search for a summer internship rather than a traditional summer job. When people hear the word internship, many people assume an internship is unpaid work. This is not always the case. According to a 2006 survey, 84% of American college students reported having an internship during some point in college and 64% of those students said they were paid for their work. Many internships will pay students stipends, often times more than what you would earn in a traditional summer job. Most of the time, paying internships come from established internship programs at large companies, and usually there is an association to high-paying industries and high-paying internships. Finance internships at investment banks or venture capital firms, for example, are typically the best paying offering summer interns as much as $14,000 for one summer of work. Of course, these internships also tend to be the most competitive to get, and successful applicants usually need to demonstrate an interest in this field through their coursework and/or extracurricular activities. Some firms also will only consider students from elite colleges although some will occasionally make exceptions for stellar students from second tier institutions. Management consulting internships also pay well as do some engineering internships. Internships in the nonprofit world, the arts, and for government organizations will most likely not pay. However, if you have an interest in a field that is unlikely to be able to pay you directly, you may want to check with your college to see if they offer any grants or fellowships for students who want to get a non-paying summer internships. Many colleges have programs that will distribute funds to you to compensate you for your unpaid summer internship work. Sometimes these funds can be quite substantial allocating between $3,000 and $6,000 for a summer of full-time work. In some cases, these programs focus specifically on a certain type of internship such as public interest internships or art-related internships, but you should check with the career services office at your school to see what options they have that meet your interests.

Even if you are unable to get paid for internship work either directly through the company you are working for or through funding from your college, you should ask your college whether you are eligible to receive course credit for a summer internship. Many colleges will allow you to obtain course credit for internships related to your studies which means that your experience can reduce the number of credits you are required to take the following semester. If you college says that they will count your internship for credit, you will need to ask them whether you are required to pay for these credits or whether they will be included in the cost of your regular fall tuition. Some colleges have started to charge students for credit they earn over the summer to prevent them from losing out on the funds you would have paid them if you had earned those credits through typical coursework, but some schools will allow you to obtain these credits without paying the regular rate. If you combine credits you earn through summer internships with AP credits, you may be able to graduate a semester or a year early potentially saving you hundreds if not thousands of dollars.

One thing to keep in mind about internships is that unlike most summer jobs, they actually can be very helpful in building your resume so that you can get a job right out of college. Most employers will see internship experience at a related company as relevant, and it will give you a leg up when compared with other new graduates. According to a 2012 study by the National Association of Colleges and Employers, 64% of students who had paid internships at for-profit companies had received a job offer by graduation compared to 35.7% of students who had not participated in any internship although interestingly, the students who had unpaid internships at for-profit companies only fared marginally better than the general population with 37.1% receiving jobs by graduation. The study also revealed that the average unpaid intern spent more time on clerical duties than paid interns who spent more time working on essential functions which may account for some of the difference in job offer rates. Making sure that the internship you select will give you useful and relevant experience may be critical in assessing its value in terms of getting a job offer.

Many students are offered job offers directly from the companies they intern for at the end of the summer. This is more likely to happen when you participate in an established internship program where it has become an established practice to recruit new employees from the intern pool. You should ask your career services departments which companies have hired students from your school in the past after completing internships. Getting a job offer at the internship is nice enough, but in some cases, companies will even offer you a signing bonus for committing to work for the company within a few days of the time they make the offer. Taking the offer will prevent you from searching for other jobs during your senior year, but it can give you a nice payout. Signing bonuses for entry-level positions can range from a few hundred dollars to up to $6,000 for jobs in high-paying industries such as finance.

Keep in mind that once you earn $6,130 during the year (your work-study earnings are not included in this number), each additional dollar that you earn will increase your Expected Family Contribution by 50 cents. Like all earnings, you will be required to report any earnings from summer jobs or internships to your college, and if you earn any more than $6,130, each additional dollar is only half as valuable.

Key Points

- Internships are often preferable to traditional summer jobs.
- Many internships are paid.
- You can also get money for unpaid internships through grant programs distributed through your college. When you spend your summer living at home or with family, you may be able to pocket these funds and use them for college the following semester.
- Internships also increase earning potential after college.
- Some colleges allow you to get course credit for internships, reducing your tuition bill the following semester (or, when combined with AP credits, may allow you to graduate early).
- Successful internships may also result in a job offer, occasionally with a signing bonus distributed at the beginning of your senior year (most frequently offered in high-paying industries such as management consulting , tech, and finance).

Potential Savings

- $2,000-$14,000 for a full-time summer internship.
- Up to $6,000 in summer internship grants from universities.
- Up to $5,000 for signing bonuses.

Chapter 13
Live Off Campus

When you imagine your life in college, you likely imagine living in a dorm room and eating in a dining hall. This is a fundamental part of many students' vision of in college, and for good reason. Living on campus comes with all sorts of benefits. There likely won't be another time in your life when you'll have to chance to live in a building with hundreds of residents exactly your age. And dorm life between late night conversations, parties, and group study sessions can be a lot of fun. Many students end up meeting some of their best lifelong friends in dorms. And there are practical benefits too. If something breaks, someone comes to fix it with a simple call, you don't have to clean the bathrooms, there's no monthly rent to worry about paying on time, no utility bills, you probably have a minimal commute to class, and you don't have to burden yourself with grocery shopping or cooking. Between all of these things, there is a lot of reason why you might want to consider living in a dorm. But at an average of $10,000 per year and in some cases up to $15,000 (and in one egregious example over $18,000 annually) including board, dorm life is not cheap.

If you go to college in an expensive city like New York City or Boston, living off-campus might not be much cheaper, but in many parts of the country, off-campus housing could save you up to $6,000 per year (or $24,000 by the end of college). And if you have the opportunity to live with relatives and skip out on rent altogether, forgoing the on-campus experience could mean major savings of approximately $40,000 by graduation at the average school (and up to $60,000 at some of the most expensive ones).

These days, many colleges will require all first-year students to live on-campus. And because of all the aforementioned benefits of on-campus housing, it isn't a bad requirement. A year or even two on campus can give you the chance to meet a core group of friends and get the dorm experience. Still, choosing to move off-campus as an upperclassmen and transitioning to living in an apartment or house shared with friends can save you money while allowing you to maintain your college social life at the same time. You'll have to take up some of the burdens of independent life such as cooking, cleaning, and paying rent and utility bills each month, but the cost savings may make all of that worth it. It really comes down to how much you'll save. This varies dramatically from school to school. In real estate, everything comes down to location. The neighborhoods immediately surrounding your college are likely where you'll want to live. I recommend doing your research on the local rental rates before choosing a college so you have an idea of what you can expect to pay for housing. Go to Craigslist and look for apartment listings near each school on your list. Or, email the college's housing office to see if they have a list of local listings (many colleges have a network of landlords that list their properties with them). Remember that apartments can be shared. If you find a three bedroom apartment, you can divide the rent by three or even four if one of you is willing to share a bedroom. You might be surprised how much money you'll save when you compare the local rates to the college rates, and doing this exercise may also help you better understand the actual cost differences when you compare one college to the next.

The decision to live off-campus is not for everyone. For some students, the convenience and social advantages of living on campus far outweigh the financial savings you might get from moving to an off-campus option. There are many other ways to save money in college so this strategy is by no means essential for all money-minded students. Still, if you are flexible, you might find that moving off campus can be a great way to save money and be an exciting adventure at the same time.

Key Points

- You may want to live on-campus for social reasons and for convenience.
- Living off campus, even for just a couple years of college, can save you thousands of dollars.
- The location of your school and the real estate prices in surrounding neighborhoods will determine the cost of renting an apartment and can vary considerably from school to school.
- It is best to research real estate prices before choosing a college to understand your approximate housing costs over four years.

Potential Savings

- Up to $32,000-$60,000 ($8,000-$10,000 per year) for commuters all four years.

- Up to $12,000-$24,000 ($3,000-$6,000 per year) for students living off campus all four years.
- Up to $6,000-$12,000 ($3,000-$6,000 per year) for students who live off campus the last two years of college.

Chapter 14
Negotiate

If you are unhappy with your financial aid package, you should make a request for it to be reevaluated. Determining financial aid packages is not a science. There is an element of subjectivity involved, and this is where negotiation comes into play.

Many colleges have a general formula for determining financial aid, but most also have some wiggle room money which they can allocate to students who they really want or to students who have financial circumstances that may not be reflected in the FAFSA or CSS Profile.

If you are dissatisfied with your aid package, you should call up the financial aid office at the college and request that they reevaluate your package. Some schools will not allow a reevaluation, but many will especially if you give them one of the following reasons:

Another School Gave You a Better Package

If you received a better financial aid offer from another school, you should alert the school you are hoping to negotiate with and offer to send them the other school's offer. Some schools have a policy of matching your best offer and many schools will at least meet you partway. Reiterating to the financial aid office that this school is your first choice and that you will attend if they are able to provide you with an equivalent aid package may provide them the added incentive to devote some of their flex pile of money to you.

Your Financial Circumstances Have Changed

If anyone in your family has lost their job or if the value of your investments has decreased since you originally applied for financial aid, this is a perfect reason to ask for a reevaluation. Even if there hasn't been a material change in your finances yet, but if you project that your family might have a circumstance change soon because of a health problem in the family that is likely to decline and affect earnings or mass layoffs at one of your parents' companies, you may want to bring this up as a reason why you want your package to be reconsidered. Financial uncertainty can be a perfectly acceptable reason to be hesitant to a commit to a school and expressing these concerns can sometimes help you secure additional funds.

Financial Circumstances Were not Included in Your FAFSA or CSS Profile

The FAFSA and CSS Profile try to gauge your family's ability to pay for college, but they do not cover everything. These forms tend to focus on income and assets while minimizing the importance of expenses. They will ask you if your family has any additional children in college, but other major life expenses such as paying for a nursing home for a grandparent or extended family member may not be accounted for. If there are circumstances in your life that require your family to spend more than the average household, you should let the financial aid office know and ask them to reevaluate your aid application having taken these expenses into account.

You Won't Be Able to Attend Because of Finances

Everyone has a maximum amount they are willing to pay for college, and you may also have a maximum amount you are comfortable taking out in loans. If your package does not fit this criteria you've laid out for yourself, you may decide you can't afford to go. If this is the case for you, telling a college bluntly that you would love to attend their school but just can't afford it based on the package they've offered you, they may be able to help you out. In the best case scenario, they may offer you more grant money to help cover any shortfall. Alternatively, they may help you secure an on-campus job (even if you didn't qualify through the Federal Work-Study Program) or help you find scholarships you might be eligible for. If you choose to ask for a financial aid reevaluation based on your inability to pay, your approach is important. Instead of being adversarial, the best way to bring this up is to call the financial aid office and simply ask if they can help you. Tell them how much you'd like to attend their institution and how you've reworked the numbers multiple times but can't find a way to make the numbers work. Lay out the specifics and then ask them if they have any ideas on how to help you. Financial aid officers often went into this profession because they wanted to help students go to college. They generally want to make the institution affordable you if they can and will be especially motivated to extend themselves if you approach them by asking for their help rather than attacking their initial offer.

Regardless of the reason you ask for a reevaluation from the list above, one thing to keep in mind is that it is always helpful to have the student make this call rather than the parent. While it may be a good idea to have a parent on the phone to make sure any specific financial aid questions are being answered, a student's presence can make a huge difference. If as a student you come across as highly motivated, ambitious, and excited about attending their institution, you will make it much more likely that the financial aid officer will take an interest in you and want to fight for your case. This is not only human nature, but it is smart. A student who really wants to be at a particular college is more likely to stay at that school and succeed. If an aid officer believes in you, they are more likely to fight for a bigger slice of their limited resources to be allocated to you.

Key Points

- Your financial aid award is not set in stone.
- Talking to the financial aid office and being open about your reasons for wanting them to take a second look at your offer are the best way to get a reevaluation.
- Students are often more effective at convincing financial aid offices to give more money than parents although approaching the aid office together is also fine.

Potential Savings

- Thousands of dollars (in some cases up to $10,000 per year or even more).

Chapter 15
Watch Out for Declining Aid Packages

As you sit and review your financial aid offer, you might be inclined to look at the dollar amount for student loans and multiply it by four for the number of years you plan to be in college. For instance, let's say that your aid package requires you to take out $4,000 in loans. You see this and estimate that by graduation, you will have a total of $16,000 in loans (i.e. $4,000 x 4 years =$16,000). This logic makes sense, but you have to be careful. There is a pervasive practice called **front-loading** which means offering students substantially more generous aid package during their freshman year and then reducing it each subsequent year. Although this practice happens to varying degrees at different schools, you will find that it happens to some extent at the vast majority. Offering generous aid packages to entering freshmen lures students in, and once students are part of the way through their educations, it becomes substantially more difficult for them to leave, reducing a college's incentive to offer equally generous aid.

Many students find that not only does the base tuition of their college increase each year, but the value of the institutional need-based grants they are offered, merit aid, and the percentage of need met will often decrease even if their family's financial situation has remained unchanged. Because you are only offered one year's financial aid package at a time, it is difficult to do financial planning as a freshman and determine how much in loans you will be eventually required to take out. The best strategy is to try to figure out how much the average financial aid package drops off by.

You can look up the average financial aid package for freshmen at any given school and then compare that to the average aid package offered to all students. You will also be able to see the average percent of need meet for freshmen versus all students as well as average merit-based gift and the precent of students receiving it for freshmen versus all students. You will see that the aid package for all students is almost always lower than the aid package offered to freshmen, but by varying degrees at each school. Checking for the type of drop off at each school on your list will help you determine how much you can actually expect to pay. Here are a few examples:

New York University

Average Freshman Grant: $31,857
Average Grant (all students): $27,544
Merit Aid (freshman): 9.2%
Merit Aid (all students): 5.6%

Syracuse University

Average Freshman Grant: $34,700
Average Grant (all students): $32,540
Merit Aid (freshman): 6.7%
Merit Aid (all students): 6%

Northeastern University

Average Freshman Grant: $29,108
Average Grant (all students): $24,099
Merit Aid (freshman): 40%
Merit Aid (all students): 34.6%

As you can see from the list above, these schools have a noticeable drop off both in the amount of aid given to freshman and upperclassmen and in the percentage of students granted merit aid between freshman and later years. You can find all of this information on CollegeData (http://www.collegedata.com) which allows you to look up each school on your list and see a detailed breakdown of their financial aid awards in their "Money Matters" section.

You may also want to take a look at a list of tuition guarantee schools (Chapter 19). While these schools may still engage in the practice of front-loading, they will at least guarantee that the base tuition rate stays the same during all four years of college meaning that while your aid package may decrease each year, at least the base tuition rate will be fixed.

Key Points

• Research each college on your list to figure out whether they engage in front-loading, and the average amount aid packages drop off.
• Be upfront with your concerns about front-loading to the financial aid staff when evaluating your aid package, and if possible, try to get any response from

them about any grants or scholarships that they guarantee will renew the following year in writing.

• Consider tuition guarantee schools for more price predictability.

Chapter 16
Pick Schools with Generous Merit Aid

(especially if you don't quality for need-based aid)

Colleges offering generous merit aid can be a great way to reduce the net cost of college for any student, although students who do not qualify for need-based aid benefit the most from merit aid. For a student in a high income bracket, merit aid is one of the easiest ways to reduce the net cost of tuition. Every dollar you earn in merit aid is one fewer dollar you need to pay the college each semester. And if you don't qualify for need-based aid, merit scholarships are the only way to get financial aid directly from an institution so it is often the first line of defense.

If you do qualify for need-based aid, merit aid can still be a good component of your money-saving strategies, but you need to make sure you understand how it works and its limitations. Students with financial need can benefit from merit scholarships, but perhaps to a slightly lesser extent than for students without need. As we discussed in the outside scholarship section, merit aid will reduce a student's need-based aid package before it reduces your out of pocket expenses. Depending on the college, the way that your aid package is reduced may vary. Some schools will reduce or eliminate the value of your student loans and work-study obligations first (which is the ideal scenario), but other schools may start by reducing your college's institutional grant money. So, for example, if you receive a $4,000 merit scholarship and the original need-based aid package included loans amounting to $5,500 and an institutional grant equivalent to $10,000, some schools will reduce your loan amount to $1,500 and keep your grant at $10,000 while others may still say you need to take out $5,500 and reduce your grant to $6,000. In the latter case, you can see that the actual benefit to you of getting a merit scholarship amount to nothing since you would have been getting gift money you were not required to pay back with or without the merit-based award. The good news is that most colleges will at least meet you in the middle, and while your grant aid may be slightly reduced with a merit award, you will still likely get some reduction in loans or work-study (especially if you talk to the financial aid office and try to negotiate). Of course, you can also get merit scholarships that exceed that value of your demonstrated need. Once this happens, you will actually start to reduce the amount of money you are required to pay out of pocket each semester. So, let's say you get a $20,000 scholarship, and we use the same example as we did above and say you have a $5,500 loan in your financial aid package and a $10,000 grant. In this case, the grant money and loan money would disappear, but you'd still have $4,500 left which you could use to directly reduce your out of pocket expenses. As a student with financial need, the merit scholarships that will help you the most are high value merit scholarships that will exceed the amount of your need. The scholarships in Chapters 24 and Chapter 26 are great places to look.

For students who do not qualify for need-based aid, all

scholarship amounts equal cost savings and any merit scholarship is generally helpful. Looking for colleges that give scholarships to a large percentage of students who do not receive need-based aid can be great additions to your college list. The colleges below offer merit-based scholarships to at least one quarter of their students who do not qualify for need-based financial aid. This list, based on data from *US News and World Report*, excludes athletic awards and tuition benefits.

Colleges With High Percentage of Students Without Need Receiving Merit Aid

100% - **Frank Lloyd Wright School of Architecture** - Scottsdale, AZ

79% - **Webb Institute** - Glen Cove, NY

72% - **Cooper Union** - New York, NY

49% - **Hillsdale College** - Hillsdale, MI

48% - **Furman University** - Greenville, SC

48% - **Franklin W. Olin College of Engineering** - Needham, MA

47% - **School of the Art Institute of Chicago** - Chicago, IL

45% - **Denison University** - Granville, OH

43% - **Samford University** - Birmingham, AL

42% - **Trinity University** - San Antonio, TX

41% - **SUNY College Oneonta** - Oneonta, NY

41% - **New England Conservatory of Music** - Boston, MA

40% - **University of Tulsa** - Tulsa, OK

40% - **Millsaps College** - Jackson, MS

39% - **College of Wooster** - Wooster, OH

39% - **Rhodes College** - Memphis, TN

38% - **Marquette University** - Milwaukee, WI

38% - **Grace College and Seminary** - Winona Lake, IN

38% - **University of Denver** - Denver, CO

38% - **University of Dayton** - Dayton, OH

38% - **Gonzaga University** - Spokane, WA

38% - **St. Mary's College** - Notre Dame, IN

38% - **Mississippi College** - Clinton, MS

37% - **Hendrix College** - Conway, AR

37% - **Lindenwood University** - St. Charles, MO

37% - **Centre College-** Danville, KY

36% - **Ouachita Baptist University** - Arkadelphia, AR

36% - **Oberlin College** - Oberlin, OH

36% - **Augustana College** - Sioux Falls, SD

36% - **Eckerd College** - St. Petersburg, FL

36% - **Southeastern Oklahoma State University** - Weathersford, OK

35% - **Truman State University** - Kirksville, MO

34% - **Muhlenberg College** - Allentown, PA

34% - **New Mexico Institute of Mining and Technology** - Socorro, NM

34% - **Carroll College** - Helena, MT

34% - **Savannah College of Art and Design** - Savannah, GA

34% - **Washington College** - Chestertown, MD

33% - **Illinois Institute of Technology** - Chicago, IL

33% - **Tulane University** - New Orleans, LA

33% - **Hampden-Sydney College** - Hampden-Sydney, VA

33% - **Drake University** - Des Moines, IA

33% - **Rose-Hulman Institute of Technology** - Terre Haute, IN

33% - **Willamette University** - Salem, OR

33% - **Illinois Wesleyan University** - Bloomington, IL

33% - **Menlo College** - Atherton, CA

33% - **Southwestern University** - Georgetown, TX

33% - **Baylor University** - Waco, TX

32% - **Southern Utah University** - Cedar City, UT

32% - **University of Dallas** - Irving, TX

32% - **New College of Florida** - Sarasota, FL

32% - **Westminster College** - Salt Lake City, UT

32% - **Creighton University** - Omaha, NE

32% - **California Lutheran University** - Thousand Oaks, CA

32% - **Lawrence University** - Appleton, WI

32% - **Calvin College** - Grand Rapids, MI

32% - **Southern Methodist University** - Dallas, TX

32% - **Transylvania University** - Lexington, KY

31% - **Wesleyan College** - Macon, GA

31% - **University of South Carolina** - Columbia, SC

31% - **St. Lawrence University** - Canton, NY

31% - **University of Jamestown** - Jamestown, ND

31% - **St. Joseph's University** - Philadelphia, PA

31% - **Abilene Christian University** - Abilene, TX

31% - **University of Rochester** - Rochester, NY

31% - **San Francisco Art Institute** - San Francisco, CA

30% - **The Catholic University of America** - Washington, DC

30% - **Covenant College** - Lookout Mountain, GA

30% - **Juniata College** - Huntingdon, PA

30% - **Clark University** - Worcester, MA

30% - **Loyola University New Orleans** - New Orleans, LA

30% - **University of Portland** - Portland, OR

30% - **Iowa State University** - Ames, IA

29% - **Whitman College** - Walla Walla, WA

29% - **Kalamazoo College** - Kalamazoo, MI

29% - **Miami University** - Oxford - Oxford, OH

28% - **Webber International University** - Babson Park, FL

28% - **Westmont College** - Santa Barbara, CA

28% - **Hobart and William Smith Colleges** - Geneva, NY

28% - **St. Michael's College** - Colchester, VT

28% - **University of Tampa** - Tampa, FL

28% - **Albion College** - Albion, MI

28% - **Taylor University** - Upland, IN

28% - **Bennington College** - Bennington, VT

28% - **Ohio Wesleyan University** - Delaware, OH

27% - **Indiana University Bloomington** - Bloomington, IN

27% - **Monmouth University** - West Long Branch, NJ

27% - **St. Louis University** - St. Louis, MO

27% - **University of Puget Sound** - Tacoma, WA

27% - **Lipscomb University** - Nashville, TN

27% - **Stonehill College** - Easton, MA

27% - **St. John's University** - Collegeville, MN

27% - **Queens University of Charlotte** - Charlotte, NC

27% - **Hope College** - Holland, MI

26% - **Northeastern University** - Boston, MA

26% - **Duquensne University** - Pittsburgh, PA

26% - **Rensselaer Polytechnic Institute** - Troy, NY

26% - **University of Vermont** - Burlington, VT

26% - **Beloit College** - Beloit, WI

Key Points

- A student admitted to any school on the list above has a good chance of receiving a merit scholarship.
- For a high income student, applying to the schools on the list above may be one of the easiest ways to reduce the net cost of attendance.

Potential Savings

- Up to $20,000-$250,000 over the course of four years when compared to a similarly priced college not offering merit aid. Savings are typically greatest for students who do not qualify for need-based aid who may not get any aid at all at comparable schools not offering merit aid options.

Chapter 17
Consider No Loan Schools

One of the best ways to graduate from college with no debt is to seek out a no loan school. No loan schools are colleges that have made a   commitment to providing students with financial aid packages that do not include loans. This means that while you may still have a parental contribution, student contribution, and/or work-study plan, any additional need will be covered by grants. As a result, your potential savings are huge. You don't have to pay grant money back so choosing a school that does not include student loans in its financial aid packages could end up saving you many thousands of dollars in the long run completely eliminating any obligations to pay anything after college.

Of course, very few colleges have the resources to implement this kind of a plan for all of its students. There are only 16 colleges and universities that have a no loan policy that applies to every admitted student. All of these schools are highly selective which means that they are more realistic options for students with outstanding academic records. Still, there are a number of other colleges and universities that have made a no loan commitment to some percentage of the student body usually restricted to students who earn below a certain income threshold and/or who are from a particular part of the country. Not all of these options are highly competitive academically so there are opportunities for low income students with mediocre academic records to attend a no loan college as well.

An important thing to understand is that just because you decide to attend a no loan college does not necessarily mean you will not end up taking out any loans. Your aid package may still include a student contribution, work-study requirement, and a parental contribution. Some students at no loan schools will still opt to take out loans so that they can reduce their contributions, work fewer hours, or reduce the burden on their parents to pay the EFC. Still, choosing to attend a no loan school will likely significantly reduce if not entirely eliminate any potential college debt and are a great option for students who qualify.

<u>No Loan Schools for Everyone</u>

The following colleges do not include any loans in their financial aid packages. These schools have made a commitment to replace all loans with grants and work-study programs for all students regardless of family income or state residency. Most of these colleges are highly competitive and are most realistic for students with outstanding academic and extracurricular records.

Colleges with Universal No Loan Policy

Amherst College
Bowdoin College
Claremont McKenna College
Colby College
Columbia University

Davidson College
Haverford College
Harvard University
Pomona College
Princeton University
Stanford University
Swarthmore College
University of Pennsylvania
Vanderbilt University
Washington and Lee
Yale University

No Loan Schools for Low Income Students

There are also a number of schools that have eliminated loans for low income students. Below, you will find a list of schools who offer no loan aid packages to students whose families earn below a certain income threshold. Most of these colleges are also highly competitive and primarily serve students with strong high school academic and extracurricular records.

Brown University - Students whose families earn below $100,000 per year

California Institute of Technology (Caltech) - US students with family income under $60,000 per year

Connecticut College - Students with income under $50,000 or EFC under $5,000 per year

Cornell University - Students with family incomes under $60,000 per year

Dartmouth College - Students with family incomes under $100,000 receive full tuition grants

Duke University - Students with family incomes under $40,000 per year

Emory University - Students with family incomes under $50,000 per year

Kenyon College - Available to the 25 students with the greatest financial need

Lafayette College - Students from families earning less than $50,000 per year

Lehigh University - Students from families with incomes less than $50,000 per year

Massachusetts Institute of Technology - Students with family incomes under $75,000 per year. However, MIT has a pretty high self-help expectation (work-study and outside scholarships) of $6,000 which has required some students to take out loans to cover some or all of this amount.

Northwestern University - Students with the greatest financial need. Majority will have incomes under $55,000. Students are required to be eligible for the Pell Grant and have need greater than 80% of the cost of attendance.

Oberlin College - Students who are eligible for the Pell Grant

Rice University - Students who have family incomes

under $80,000

Tufts University - Students whose families earn under $40,000

University of Chicago - Students whose families earn under $60,000 in income.

University of North Carolina at Chapel Hill - Students whose families earn up to 200% of the Federal Poverty Line and who are enrolled full-time

Vassar College - Students whose family incomes are below $60,000 per year

Washington University in St. Louis - Students with family incomes below $60,000 per year

Wellesley University - Students with family incomes below $60,000 per year

Wesleyan University - Students with family incomes below $40,000 per year

Williams College - Williams once had a no loan policy for all students, but they had to revoke it a few years back due to financial difficulties. Some no loan packages are still available to low income students.

Regional No Loan Schools

In addition to these schools, there are additional schools that offer no loan financial aid packages for students from a particular regional area and who meet income qualifications. You can find a list of these colleges and universities and the regional requirement below. Not all of these schools are not highly competitive from an admissions perspective, and many of these can be realistic options for students with mediocre academic records.

Appalachian State University - North Carolina residents entering as full-time freshmen students with incomes below the Federal Poverty Line

Arizona State University - Arizona residents entering freshman year with income up to $42,500 who are eligible to receive the Pell Grant. Students must also meet all course competencies and at least one aptitude requirement for admission described in their Freshman Admissions Requirements (https://students.asu.edu/admission/competencies).

Boston University - Boston residents who graduate from the Boston Public Schools. Students must submit the FAFSA and CSS Profile by February 15th).

Colorado State University - Pueblo - Colorado undergrads who qualify for the Pell grant and who have family AGI $57,000 or less *may* be eligible for a no loan plan.

Fairfield University - Students from Bridgeport Public Schools and diocesan high schools with family incomes below $50,000 receive full tuition grants.

Georgia Institute of Technology - Georgia residents with family incomes below $33,3000 and eligible to file a

1040A or 1040 E2. Students are required to maintain a 2.0 GPA minimum.

Indiana University - Bloomington - Indiana residents who complete 21st Century Scholars Application in middle school which requires them to pledge to remain drug-, alcohol-, and crime-free and to maintain a 2.0 GPA). They also must be low income (eligible for the Federal School Lunch Program) and plan to enroll full-time in university.

Lamar University - Texas residents eligible for the Pell Grant and who have incomes under $25,000 receive full tuition and fees in grants. Students are also required to maintain an adequate academic record.

Miami University (Ohio) - Ohio residents from families earning less than $35,000 per year receive full tuition and fees. Students must submit FAFSA by February 15th and must be enrolled full-time. Students must also maintain "satisfactory academic progress."

Michigan State University - Michigan residents who are income with family incomes below the Federal Poverty Line. Students must be eligible for Pell Grants and be enrolled full-time.

North Carolina State University - North Carolina residents with family incomes less than 150% of the Federal Poverty Line and "limited assets"

Sacred Heart University - Students from Fairfield County, Connecticut high schools and income under

$50,000 receive full tuition

University of Texas - Dallas - Texas residents who are Pell grant eligible with under $25,000 in family income receive full tuition and fees. Students must be enrolled full-time and maintain a 2.5 GPA.

Texas A&M University - Residents of Texas with AGI under $60,000. Students must maintain a 2.5 GPA and be enrolled full-time. The FAFSA must also be submitted by March 15th.

Texas State University - San Marcos - Texas residents whose families earn under $25,000 in AGI ($35,000 for graduates of San Marcos high school). Students must also submit their FAFSA by April 1st and maintain a 2.0 GPA.

University of California System - California residents with a family income under $80,000 who submit their FAFSA by March 2nd. Available for the first four years as a UC undergrad for students who enroll as freshmen or two years for transfer students. Students must be enrolled at least half-time.

University of Florida - Florida residents with family incomes under $40,000 and whose parents did not earn a college degree

University of Illinois at Urbana-Champaign - Illinois residents with zero EFC and income below the Federal Poverty Line

University of Louisville - Kentucky residents with a family income below 150% of the Federal Poverty Line

University of Maryland at College Park - Maryland students with zero EFC

University of Michigan at Ann Arbor - Michigan residents with zero EFC who are pursuing a first bachelor's degree

University of Tennessee - The Pledge Scholarship is available to Tennessee residents with under $40,000 in family income (approximately 200% of the Federal Poverty Line) and who maintain a GPA of 2.0. Applications must be submitted by December 1st and the FAFSA by February 15th.

University of Texas at El Paso - Students who are Texas residents with under $30,000 in family income receive full tuition in grants. Students must qualify for in-state tuition and must be enrolled in 30 credit hours/yr or more with a 2.0 GPA or higher.

University of Toledo - Students who graduate from one of six Ohio districts (Akron, Cincinnati, Cleveland, Columbus, Dayton, or Toledo) with a 3.0 or higher receive full tuition in grants. Students must also be eligible for the Pell Grant.

University of Vermont - Students must be residents of Vermont and Pell-eligible.

Key Points

- No loan schools will not put loans include any loans in your financial aid package.
- No loan schools may still include a student contribution that you believe is unrealistic so some students who attend these schools still end up taking out (usually small) loans to cover this part of their package.

Potential Savings

- Eliminates or significantly reduces loans, replacing them with grants.
- Up to the value of full tuition, in some cases $250,000 over four years.

Chapter 18
Select Schools That Meet 100% of Need

In an ideal world, colleges would offer 100% of their admitted students enough financial aid so that students' families wouldn't have to pay any more than their EFC. Unfortunately, most colleges do not have the resources to make that happen resulting in financial aid packages that include "unmet need." It is up to a student to figure out where this money will come from, but in many cases the result is private loans. The list below includes the colleges which guarantee that they will meet 100% of demonstrated need.

While the aid package they give you may still include federal loans and work study, they will make sure that between institutional grants and your EFC, there is no leftover unmet need that you'll eventually need to account for via more student loans. Attending one of these schools will not keep you out of debt necessarily, but it can significantly limit the amount of loans you need to take out. Keep in mind, however, that schools not on this list may still cover 100% of your demonstrated need or at least very close to it. There are many colleges that offer packages that come close offering 100% of demonstrated need for some students but perhaps not all students, with average aid packages meeting 95% or more of demonstrated need. Of course there are also colleges on the other side of the spectrum with packages meeting under 70% of need. If you would like to see the average percentage of need is met for any given school, you can find that data available on CollegeData (http://www.collegedata.com).

Here are the colleges that guarantee that all students will have their full need met:

Amherst College
Barnard College
Bates College
Boston College
Bowdoin College
Brown University
Bryn Mawr
California Institute of Technology
Carleton College
Claremont McKenna College
Colby College
Colgate University
College of the Holy Cross
Columbia University
Cornell University
Dartmouth College
Davidson College
Duke University
Franklin and Marshall College
Emory University
Georgetown University
Gettysburg College
Grinnell College
Hamilton College

Harvard University
Harvey Mudd College
Haverford College
Macalester College
Massachusetts Institute of Technology
Middlebury College
Mount Holyoke College
Northwestern University
Oberlin College
Occidental College
Pitzer College
Pomona College
Princeton University
Rice University
Scripps College
Smith College
St. Olaf College
Stanford University
Swarthmore College
Thomas Aquinas College
Trinity College
Tufts University
University of Chicago
University of North Carolina – Chapel Hill
University of Notre Dame
University of Pennsylvania
University of Richmond
University of Southern California
University of Virginia
Vanderbilt University
Vassar College
Washington and Lee University
Washington University in St. Louis
Wellesley College

Wesleyan University
Williams College
Yale University

Key Points

- Colleges that meet 100% of demonstrated need eliminate "unmet need" from your aid package including private loans and PLUS loans.
- You may still need to take out federal loans (unless the college also appears on the list of no loan schools in Chapter 17).
- There are other schools not on this list that still meet 90% or more of demonstrated need. You can find this information on CollegeData (http://www.collegedata.com).

Potential Savings

- Up to $40,000-$80,000 over four years when unmet need is eliminated.

Chapter 19
Choose a Tuition Guarantee Plan

The vast majority of colleges reserve the right to increase the cost of tuition each year you attend, and many of them do. This year, the average private college increased its tuition rate by 3.7% and the average public college by 2.9%. These are not small figures when you factor in that you might experience these sorts of increases each year you are in college. And just because the cost of tuition goes up, doesn't mean your financial aid package goes up. Usually it doesn't. At many schools, tuition increases do not end up increasing your scholarship or grant money, but rather just increase your loans from year to year. So let's look at an example. Let's say the base total cost of attendance at a college is $65,000 when you enroll as a freshman. Let's also say you have an EFC of $25,000, $3,000 in work-study, and part of your financial aid package includes a $30,000 institutional grant from the college.

Year 1
EFC: $25,000
Work-Study: $3,000
Grant: $30,000
Loans: $7,000
Total Cost Year 1: $65,000

Between your freshman and sophomore years, there is a

cost increase of 3.7% and your EFC, work-study, and institutional grant stays the same (although keep in mind that realistically, institutional grants are often reduced after freshman year).

Year 2:
EFC: $25,000
Work-Study: $3,000
Grant: $30,000
Loans: $9,405
Total Cost Year 2: $67,405

During the next two years, your EFC remains the same and you continue to receive the same grant money and work-study each year, but the tuition continues to increase at 3.7% annually.

Year 3:
EFC: $25,000
Work-Study: $3,000
Grant: $30,000
Loans: $11,898
Total Cost Year 3: $69,898

Year 4:
EFC: $25,000
Work-Study: $3,000
Grant: $30,000
Loans: $14,485
Total Cost Year 4: $72,485

What you can see in the above example is that a student could conceivable get their freshman aid package, see that they would be expected to take out $7,000 in loans and assume that this meant that by senior year they should have $28,000 in student loans. Instead, though, with the tuition increases, the student would actually end up graduating with $42,788 in loans, a difference of $14,788 before you add in all of the potential interest payments on that amount.

A tuition increase of a few percentage points may seem small, but it can end up costing you lots of money. It is a good idea to see what kind of tuition increases the colleges on your list have had in the past and whether it is something they do every year, every few years, or if they have any tuition freeze or tuition guarantee policies. A tuition freeze is when a college says that they will not raise their tuition for the time being. It could be two years or five years depending on the school and the circumstance. Colleges that are currently in a tuition freeze may provide you some assurance, but the down side is that you don't necessarily know when they will come out of the freeze, and their tuition rate having not changed in several or more years can sometimes increase significantly after a tuition free.

The better option over schools with tuition freezes are schools with a tuition guarantee (also known as a tuition lock). A tuition guarantee is when a college gives all incoming freshman a tuition rate and promises to keep that rate the same for them during all four years of college even if the official price of tuition increases. It is important to keep in mind that a tuition guarantee does not mean that your financial aid package will remain the same each year. Your aid package may still be reduced from year to year (meaning that some of these schools still engage in the practice of front-loading like many colleges), but the guarantee that your tuition will not rise helps make financial planning much easier. Some of the schools on the list below guarantee a tuition lock for all entering students. Others require students to select a tuition guarantee plan which usually locks in your tuition at a higher rate than the published price during your freshman year but gives you a rate that is forecast to be significantly lower than the price tag during your senior year, resulting in net savings over four years. You can find each college's specific policy on the links below.

Alaska Pacific University - Anchorage, AK
The Guaranteed Consolidated Tuition Plan

Angelo State University - San Angelo, TX
Fixed Tuition Plan

Andrews University - Berrien Springs, MI
Tuition Guarantee Plan

Austin State University - Austin, TX
Fixed-Rate Tuition Plan

Baylor University - Waco, TX
Guaranteed Tuition Option

Berkeley College - NY and NJ locations
Tuition Freeze Policy

Capitol Technology University - Laurel, MD
Tuition Lock

Chicago State University - Chicago, IL
Four-Year Guaranteed Tuition Plan

Clearwater Christian College - Clearwater, FL
Cost Freeze Program

Cleary University - Howell and Ann Arbor, MI
Tuition Guarantee

College of St. Joseph - Rutland, VT
Provider Scholarship

Columbia College - Columbia, MO
Fixed Rate Tuition Program

Eastern Illinois University - Charleston, IL
Guaranteed Tuition Rate Plan

George Washington University - Washington DC
GW Fixed Tuition

Governors State University - University Park, IL
Tuition Guarantee

Hardin-Simmons University - Abilene, TX
Tuition Guarantee

Hiram College - Hiram, OH
The Hiram College Tuition Guarantee

Huntingdon College - Montgomery, AL
Fixed Tuition

Illinois State University - Normal, IL
Frozen Tuition Rates

Immaculata University - Immaculata, PA
Fixed Tuition

Kettering University - Flint, MI
Fixed-Tuition Guarantee

Lamar University - Beaumont, TX
Guaranteed Price Plan

Midwestern State University - Wichita Falls, TX
Fixed Rate Designated Tuition Plans

New Saint Andrews College - Moscow, ID
Tuition Lock

Nordland College - Ashland, WI
The Nordland Tuition Guarantee

Northeastern Illinois University - Chicago, IL
Tuition Guarantee Plan

Northern Illinois University - DeKalb, IL
Guaranteed Tuition

Ohio University - Athens, OH
Ohio Guarantee

Oklahoma City University - Oklahoma City, OK
Locked Rate

Prairie View A&M University - Prairie View, TX
Guaranteed Tuition Plan

Sam Houston State University - Huntsville, TX

Texas Guaranteed Tuition Plan

Sewanee - University of the South - Sewanee, TN
Four-Year Tuition Guarantee

Southern Illinois University Carbondale - Carbondale, IL
Guaranteed Tuition Stabilization Plan

Southern Illinois University Edwardsville - Edwardsville, IL
Guaranteed Tuition

Stephen F. Austin State University - Nacogdoches, TX
Fixed Rate Tuition Plan

St. Johns University - New York, NY
Fixed Rate Tuition Plan

Sull Ross State University - Eagle Pass, TX
Guaranteed Price Plan

Tarleton State University - Stephensville, TX
Guaranteed Tuition Plan

Texas A&M University - College Station, TX
Locked-Rate Tuition Policy

Texas A&M University, Central Texas - Killeen, TX
Guaranteed Tuition and Fee Plan

Texas A&M International University - Laredo, TX
The Fixed Tuition and Fee Plan

Texas A&M University, Commerce - Commerce, TX
Guaranteed Tuition Cohort Plan

Texas A&M University, Corpus Christi - Corpus Christi, TX
Guarantee Tuition and Fee Plans

Texas A&M University at Galveston - Galveston, TX
Guaranteed Tuition Plan

Texas A&M University, Kingsville - Kingsville, TX
Guaranteed Tuition and Fees

Texas A&M University, Texarkana - Texarkana, TX
Guaranteed Tuition and Fee Program

Texas Southern University - Houston, TX
Fixed Rate Tuition Plan

Texas State University - San Marcos, TX
Guaranteed Price Plan

Texas Tech University - Lubbock, TX
Fixed Tuition

Texas Women's University - Denton, Dallas, and Houston, TX
Fixed Tuition Price Plan

Thomas College - Waterville, ME
Guaranteed Tuition

University of Colorado, Boulder - Boulder, CO
Out-of-State Tuition Guarantee

University of Dayton - Dayton, OH
Four-Year Tuition Plan

University of Houston - Houston and Victoria, TX
Fixed Tuition Rate Plan

University of Illinois at Chicago - Chicago, IL
Guaranteed Tuition Plan

University of Illinois at Springfield - Springfield, IL
Guaranteed Tuition Program

University of Illinois at Urbana/Champaign - Champaign, IL
Guaranteed Tuition Plan

University of Kansas - Lawrence, KS
Tuition Compact

University of North Texas - Denton, TX
Eagle Express Tuition Plan

University of North Texas at Dallas - Dallas, TX
"Focus" Fixed Tuition Plan

University of Texas, Arlington - Arlington, TX
Fixed Rate Tuition Plan

University of Texas, Austin - Austin, TX
Longhorn Fixed Tuition

University of Texas, Dallas - Dallas, Texas
Guaranteed Tuition Plan

University of Texas, El Paso - El Paso, TX
Guaranteed Tuition Plan

University of Texas at the Permian Basin - Odessa, TX
Guaranteed Tuition Rate Plan

University of Texas, San Antonio - San Antonio, TX
Guaranteed Tuition Plan

University of Texas, Tyler - Tyler, TX
Guaranteed Tuition Rate Plan

Western Illinois University - Macomb, IL
Cost Guarantee

West Texas A&M University - Canyon, TX
Guaranteed Tuition & Fee Plan

Key Points

- Tuition increases often increase your loan amounts from year to year.
- Understanding a college's tuition increase history and policies for each school on your list is a good idea.
- Choosing a tuition guarantee school or plan can be a good way to reduce volatility and ultimately reduce student debt.

Potential Savings

- Up to $15,000 over four years.

Chapter 20
Don't Forget Tuition Free Colleges

Wouldn't it be nice to go to a college where there was no tuition? Although no tuition colleges are becoming increasingly rare, there are still a handful of colleges that give every single student admitted a full tuition scholarship. If you are looking to graduate with no debt, choosing a no tuition college can be a great option.

Some of these schools still require students to pay fees, room and board, books, and transportation and some also require students to commit to working at an on-campus job, but in almost all cases, these colleges provide excellent value to all of their students. If your family can pay these additional expenses out of pocket, great, you're good to go. If not, though, many of these colleges offer generous need-based scholarships and grants that can reduce any student payment obligation to close to nothing.

You'll notice that some of the colleges on the list below are said to have need-based admission. This means that students with high need (i.e. lower income students) are actually given preference in the applicant pool. Part of the mission of some of these schools is to educate students with high need at an affordable price. Other schools on this list do not have need-based admission, meaning their admissions process is only based off of academic and personal accomplishments. While students with lower family incomes could benefit from any of these schools, higher income students have the best chance of admission at the schools that do not take need into account.

Alice Lloyd College - Pippa Passes, KY
Need-based admission: No
Alice Lloyd College offers free tuition to students from 108 counties in Kentucky, Ohio, Tennessee, Virginia, and West Virginia. Students are required to pay for room and board ($6,740) and work 10-20 hours per week in on-campus jobs. Out of territory students are charged a total of $14,050 for tuition, room, board, and fees.

Barclay College - Haviland, KS
Need-based admission: No
Barclay is a Christian college that awards full tuition scholarships for all students. Students are still responsible for room, board, and fees (amounting to approximately $11,000 in additional expenses). There is no work requirement.

Berea College - Berea, KY
Need-based admission: Yes
Berea is a Christian college which awards every admitted student the Tuition Promise Scholarship which offers full tuition. As a part of the scholarship, students are required to work in an on-campus job. The cost of housing, meals, and fees (equal to $7,220) is not covered with this scholarship, however, the vast majority of students receive additional assistance to cover some or all of these expenses as well (the average student last year paid

$1,234 to cover all of these additional expenses).

College of the Ozarks - Point Lookout, MO
Need-based admission: Yes
The College of the Ozarks is a Christian working college which requires students to work 15 hours per week (plus two 40-hour weeks) to receive the College of the Ozarks Cost of Education Scholarship, a full tuition award. Students are responsible for room, board, and fees (approximately $6,415) although additional scholarships are offered to some students to reduce this expense. College of the Ozarks does take preference students with financial need in the admissions process.

Curtis Institute of Music - Philadelphia, PA
Need-based admission: No
Curtis Institute of Music is a four-year school that aims to educate talented musicians for careers in the liberal arts. All 165 students at Curtis receive full tuition scholarships equal to $38,728. Students are still responsible for room and board, instrument maintenance, and instructional supplies although additional aid may be available to students with need.

Deep Springs College - Inyo County, CA
Need-based admission: No
Deep Springs College is a small two-year rigorous liberal arts working college in the California desert. Deep Springs gives every student a full tuition scholarship which includes room, board, and fees. The 26 students at Deep Springs maintain a cattle herd and farm, and each students is assigned a labor position amounting to approximately 20 hours per week to make the campus self-sustaining. Currently, Deep Springs is all-male

although they are hoping to begin accepting applications from women within the next couple of years. Although the program is only two years, the majority of students transfer to a four-year college after their two years. Many Deep Springs students have gone on to top tier colleges including Harvard, Yale, and other Ivy League and equivalent institutions.

Macaulay Honors College at the City University of New York (CUNY) - New York, NY
Need-based admission: No
The Macaulay Honors College offers students with residency in New York state a full tuition scholarship as well as a computer. Although fees, room, transportation, books, supplies and food are not included (approximately $20,000), many students receive additional scholarships to help with these expenses.

US Air Force Academy - Colorado Springs, CO
Need-based admission: No
The US Air Force Academy is a military training academy that prepares graduates to become a commissioned officer for the Air Force. Students are given a full tuition scholarship including room, board, fees, transportation, and even receive a monthly stipend in exchange for a commitment post-graduation to five years of active duty service and three as inactive reserve. Applicants must be US citizens.

US Coast Guard Academy - New London, CT
Need-based admission: No
The US Coast Guard Academy is a military training academy designed to train officers for the Coast Guard. All students commit to five years post graduation serving

as a commissioned Coast Guard officer and during their time as a student receive full tuition, room, board, fees, and a living stipend of $12,000 per year.

US Merchant Marine Academy - Kings Point, NY
Need-based admission: No
The US Merchant Marine Academy is a military training academy designed to train students for careers in the maritime industry and the armed forces. Graduates commit to eight years working in the maritime industry with five years of reserve service in one unit of the armed forces or five years of active duty. Tuition, room, and board is covered by the federal government, however, students are responsible for mandatory fees, books, and transportation typically amounting to between $6,000 and $10,000 annually.

US Military Academy - West Point, NY
Need-based admission: No
The US Military Academy is a military training academy that prepares graduates to become a commissioned officer of the US Army. Students are given a full tuition scholarship including room, board, fees, and additional expenses. Students also receive a monthly stipend. Graduates have a five-year active service obligation post-graduation.

US Naval Academy - Annapolis, MD
Need-based admission: No
The US Naval Academy is a military training academy that prepares graduates to become commissioned officers for the US Navy. Students commit to five years of active duty service after graduation. Tuition, room and board are covered by the Navy and fees are deducted from a

monthly stipend awarded to each student.

Webb Institute - Glen Cove, NY
Need-based admission: No
The Webb Institute offers one academic program for all students, a double major in Naval Architecture and Marine Engineering. All 80 of its students receive a full tuition scholarship. Students are responsible for room and board, books, supplies, and transportation (approximately $19,000). Some scholarships are available to help defray the cost of these additional expenses.

Formally free colleges:

Cooper Union - New York, NY
Need-based admission: No
Cooper Union is a private four-year college located in Manhattan's East Village with an academic focus on art, architecture, and engineering. Founded in 1859, the school's mission stated that "education should be open and free to all." Due to financial difficulties, the college was forced to begin charging tuition beginning with students entering in the fall of 2014. The college now offers every entering student a 50% merit-based scholarship, amounting to $20,000 per year. Students are also responsible for fees, room, board, books and supplies. Additional need-based funds to cover tuition and other expenses are available for students with significant demonstrated need.

Olin College of Engineering - Needham, MA
Need-based admission: No
Olin is a four-year private college that admitted its first class in just 2002 but is quickly become one of the most

prestigious engineering colleges in the country. Although tiny in size, Olin students have the opportunity to cross-register at Wellesley, Babson, and Brandeis giving them ample selection in terms of course offerings. A significant endowment allowed Olin to recruit top-notch faculty, implement an innovative curriculum focused on hands-on design programs, and offer all students a full tuition scholarship. Due to significant losses during the 2008 recession, Olin was forced to reduce the full tuition to a half tuition scholarship (amounting to just over $20,000 per year) beginning with the Class of 2015. Students are responsible for fees, room, board, books, and supplies although need-based financial aid is available to students to help cover the remaining tuition and these additional expenses.

Key Points

- Free colleges can be a good option for both higher income and low income students.
- Lower income students have the most options when it comes to free colleges since some preference low income students in the admissions process.
- Some free colleges require students to work during school or complete a post-graduation working requirement.
- Formally free colleges have reduced tuition rates and can still save students money.

Potential Savings

- $50,000-$260,000 over four years.

Resources

Chapter 21
Public Schools with the Lowest Tuition

Going to an in-state institution can be a great way to spend money, but not all in-state institutions are created equal. While there are likely many reasons besides money that go into your decision of choosing a college, checking out the school in your state which offers the best in-state tuition can be worthwhile. Below you'll find the college with the lowest in-state tuition in all fifty states and the annual tuition rate as of 2014-2015.

Alabama

Alabama Agricultural and Mechanical University - $8,298

Alaska

University of Alaska, Anchorage - $6,002

Arizona

Arizona State University, Tempe - $9,811

<u>Arkansas</u>

Arkansas University of Arkansas, Pine Bluff - $5,956

<u>California</u>

California State University, Dominguez Hills - $6,099

<u>Colorado</u>

Fort Lewis College - $7,252

<u>Connecticut</u>

Central Connecticut State University - $8,877

<u>Delaware</u>

Delaware State University - $7,336

<u>Florida</u>

Florida Atlantic University - $6,039

<u>Georgia</u>

Georgia Gwinnett College - $5,353

<u>Hawaii</u>

University of Hawaii, Hilo - $7,036

Idaho

Lewis-Clark State College - $5,900

Illinois

Southern Illinois University, Edwardsville - $9,738

Indiana

Indiana University East - $6,787

Iowa

Iowa State University - $7,731

Kansas

Fort Hays State University - $4,469

Kentucky

Murray State University - $7,392

Louisiana

Louisiana State University, Alexandria - $5,315

Maine

University of Maine, Presque Isle - $7,436

Maryland

University of Maryland, Eastern Shore - $7,287

Massachusetts

Massachusetts Maritime Academy - $7,203

Michigan

Saginaw Valley State University - $8,691

Minnesota

Minnesota State University, Moorhead - $7,838

Mississippi

Mississippi University for Women - $5,640

Missouri

Missouri Southern State University - $5,416

Montana

Montana State University, Billings - $5,780

Nebraska

Wayne State College - $5,604

Nevada

University of Nevada, Reno - $6,415

New Hampshire

Plymouth State University - $12,677

New Jersey
New Jersey City University - $10,852

New Mexico

New Mexico Institute of Mining and Technology - $6,256

New York

CUNY, Hunter College - $6,129

North Carolina

Elizabeth City State University - $4,497

North Dakota

Bismarck State College - $4,222

Ohio

Shawnee State University - $7,364

Oklahoma

Northeastern State University - $4,994

Oregon

Oregon State University - $8,276

Pennsylvania

Lincoln University - $7,160

Rhode Island

Rhode Island College - $7,602

South Carolina

University of South Carolina, Beaufort - $9,092

South Dakota

Northern State University - $7,563

Tennessee

Tennessee State University - $6,776

Texas

University of Texas, Pan American - $6,134

<u>Utah</u>

Weber State University - $5,126

<u>Vermont</u>

Vermont Technical College - $13,200

<u>Virginia</u>

Virginia State University - $8,002

<u>Washington</u>

Eastern Washington University - $7,982

<u>West Virginia</u>

Fairmont State University - $5,824

<u>Wisconsin</u>

University of Wisconsin, Parkside - $7,316

Chapter 22
Regional Tuition Agreements

You know that one of the best ways to save on tuition is to attend an in-state college. Depending on where you are from and your interests, there may not be an in-state college that is a good match for you. Regional tuition agreements can be a great way to save on tuition at out-of-state schools in neighboring states. These agreements allow some students to attend public universities at the in-state rate or at least significantly lower than normal out-of-state rate. Some of these agreements are available at all students in neighboring states while others are restricted to a certain number of students or restricted based on the field you wish to study. The list includes links to each program's website where you can find out the specifics for each.

The Academic Common Market
Students who reside in one of 16 southern states are eligible to pay in-state tuition rates to study in programs not offered in their home state. The current participating states include Alabama, Arkansas, Delaware, Florida, Georgia, Kentucky, Louisiana, Maryland, Mississippi, Oklahoma, South Carolina, Tennessee, Texas, Virginia, and West Virginia.

Midwest Student Exchange Program
Students from Illinois, Indiana, Kansas, Michigan,

Missouri, Minnesota, North Dakota, and Wisconsin pay a reduced non-resident rate for tuition (usually 150% of the in-state rate) at specific programs at over 100 institutions.

New England Regional Student Program
Students from Connecticut, Maine, Massachusetts, New Hampshire, Rhode Island, and Vermont are granted in-state tuition when they enroll in a major not offered at a university in their home state. Students can enroll at any of New England's 82 public colleges and universities.

Western Interstate Commission for Higher Education (WICHE)
WICHE provides students from western states with 150% of the resident tuition rate when then enroll at one of 150 participating institutions. States included in the program include Alaska, Arizona, California, Colorado, Hawaii, Idaho, Montana, Nevada, New Mexico, North Dakota, Oregon, South Dakota, Utah, Washington, and Wyoming. This rate is not automatically awarded, and students must apply for consideration. Some institutions will only consider applicants with certain majors.

Chapter 23
Out-of-State Tuition Agreements

At some colleges, you may be able to pay in-state rates as an out-of-state student if you have a strong GPA and/or test scores. Below is a list of public universities that offer tuition waivers to excellent students and the qualifications you must have to receive the waiver. Many of these offers are only available on a first come, first served basis and are capped in number so if you are interested in one one of these programs make sure to get organized early.

Alabama

University of Alabama
UA Scholars Program
Requirements: 3.5 GPA, ACT 30 or SAT 1330 (CR+M)

University of West Alabama
Trustee Excellence Award
Requirements: 3.0 GPA, ACT of 31-36

Arkansas

Arkansas State University, Jonesboro
Undergraduate Out-of-State Scholarship
Requirements: 3.0 GPA, 24 ACT or comparable SAT score, resides in a US state

Illinois

Southern Illinois University
High Achievers Alternate Tuition Rate
Requirements: ACT 26 or SAT 1170 (CR+M) from a single administration of either test

Louisiana

Louisiana Tech University
Bulldog Out-of-State Fee Scholarship
Requirements: 2.5 GPA, ACT 23 or SAT 1050 (CR+M)

University of Louisiana, Lafayette
Out-of-State Fee Waiver
Requirements: 2.5 GPA, ACT 23 (must have a minimum of 18 verbal and 19 math) or 1050 SAT (CR + M with a minimum of 450 CR and 460 M).

University of Louisiana, Monroe
Warhawk Out-of-State Fee Waiver
Requirements: ACT 21/SAT 980 (CR+M) and 3.2 GPA, or ACT 22/SAT 1020 (CR+M) and 2.8 GPA, or ACT 23/ SAT 1060 (CR+M) and 2.5 GPA, or ACT English 18/ SAT 450 M and ACT Match 19/SAT Math 460

Michigan

University of Michigan, Dearborn
Tuition Differential Scholarship
Requirements: 3.4 GPA, ACT 24 or SAT 1100 (CR+M)

Minnesota

Minnesota State University, Moorhead
Tuition Scholarships for Non-Residents
Requirements: ACT 28 or SAT 1260 (CR+M)

Mississippi

Mississippi State University
Freshman Non-Resident Academic Excellence
Scholarship
Requirements: 3.0 GPA, ACT 22 CR+M)

University of Mississippi (Ole Miss)
Academic Excellence Award
Requirements: 3.0 GPA, ACT 32 or SAT 1400 (CR+M)

Missouri

Missouri State University
Scholarships for Out-of-State Students
Requirements: 3.7 GPA and 24 ACT/1090 SAT (CR+M)
and top 20% in class

Oklahoma

East Central University
Non-Resident Tuition Waiver
Requirements: 2.7 GPA and rank in the top 50% of class
OR 20 ACT or 940 SAT (CR+M)

Oklahoma State University
Non-Resident Achievement Scholarship
Requirements: 24 ACT or 1090 SAT (CR+M)

<u>Tennessee</u>

Tennessee State University

Academic Out-of-State Tuition Waiver Scholarship
Requirements: 3.0 GPA and ACT 21/SAT 980 (CR+M)
Academic Out-of-State Tuition Waiver Scholarship

Chapter 24
Full Tuition Scholarships

With the outrageous rates of tuition these days, there is nothing better than a full tuition scholarship. There are more out there than many people think. The problem is, there are very few centralized resources telling students where to look.

I've spent the past few weeks pulling together an extensive list of colleges that give away full tuition scholarships. Some of these schools even throw in room & board, travel expenses, books, and enrichment funding that can be used for study abroad and summer internships.

The list below includes 111 schools that offer incredible scholarships to students who demonstrate high level of achievement in their academics and/or extracurricular activities.

I have deliberately excluded scholarships which take into account the following:

- Financial need
- Winning a National Merit Scholarship
- Being a part of a specific ethnic/racial group
- Living in a specific region or state
- Planning to study a particular field

These scholarships are based entirely on merit and are open to students from around the country and in some cases the world. I highly encourage any student with competitive academic and extracurricular credentials to check them out!

Alabama

University of Alabama
Name of Scholarship: Academic Elite Scholarships
Value: Full tuition + $8,500 per year + iPad
Determining Factors: Academics, extracurriculars, service, and leadership experience
Minimum Requirements: 32 ACT or 1400 SAT, 3.8 GPA or above

Birmingham-Southern College
Name of Scholarship: Distinguished Scholars Award
Value: Up to full tuition
Determining Factors: Academic and extracurricular achievement

University of Alabama-Huntsville
Name of Scholarship: Charger Distinction Scholarship
Value: Full tuition
Determining Factors: Minimum 3.5 GPA, 1330 SAT (CR +M) or 30 ACT

Name of Scholarship: Charger Excellence Award
Value: Full tuition + housing
Determining Factors: Minimum 4.0 GPA and 1490 SAT (CR+M) or 34 ACT

University of Alabama-Birmingham
Name of Scholarship: Presidential Scholarship
Value: Full tuition
Determining Factors: 1400-1600 SAT (CR+M) or 32-36 ACT

Troy University
Name of Scholarship: The Millennium Scholar's Award
Value: Full tuition + room and board
Determining Factors: 31 ACT and/or 1380 SAT (CR+M) and minimum 3.7 GPA

Name of Scholarship: The Chancellor's Award
Value: Full tuition
Determining Factors: 27 ACT and/or 1220 SAT (M+CR) and minimum 3.5 GPA

Tuskagee University
Name of Scholarship: Distinguished Presidential Scholarship
Value: Full tuition + room and board + $800 for books
Determining Factors: 3.7 minimum GPA, 1300 SAT (CR +M) or 29 ACT

Name of Scholarship: University Merit Scholarship
Value: Full tuition + $800 for books
Determining Factors: 3.5 minimum GPA, 1180 SAT (CR +M) or 26 ACT

Alabama State University
Name of Scholarship: Presidential Scholarship
Value: Full tuition + fees, + books + room and board + $1,200 stipend for incidentals
Determining Factors: 3.76 GPA or above, 26 ACT or

1170 SAT (CR+M)

Name of Scholarship: Academic Scholarship
Value: Full tuition + fees + books + room and board
Determining Factors: 3.51 GPA or above, 25 ACT or 1090 SAT (CR+M)

Name of Scholarship: Dean's Scholarship
Value: Full tuition + fees + books
Determining Factors: 3.26 GPA or above, 22 ACT or 1020 SAT (CR+M)

Arkansas

University of Arkansas at Monticello
Name of Scholarship: Chancellor Scholarship
Value: Tuition + fees + residential stipend + board stipend
Determining Factors: 3.0 GPA or above or top 10% of high school class or 30 ACT or above

Name of Scholarship: University Scholarship
Value: Tuition + fees + residential stipend
Determining Factors: 27 ACT Composite, 19 ACT English and math, and 3.0 GPA or above

Name of Scholarship: Academic Scholarship
Value: Tuition + fees
Determining Factors: 24 ACT Composite, 19 ACT English and Math, and a 3.0 GPA or above

California

Scripps College
Name of Scholarship: New Generation Scholarship

Value: Full tuition + three flights home per year + one summer research stipend
Determining Factors: Academic performance, personal achievement, recommendations, and involvement in community and school activities
Minimum Requirements: Minimum weighted GPA of 4.0, minimum median SAT score of 1400 (CR+M)

University of Southern California
Name of Scholarship: Mork Family Scholarship
Value: Full tuition + $5,000 stipend
Awards: 10

Name of Scholarship: Stamps Leadership Scholarship
Value: Full tuition + $5,000 enrichment fund
Awards: 5
Determining Factors: Academic achievement, talent, perseverance, innovation, involvement, and leadership
Minimum Requirements: Average SAT and ACT scores in the top 1 to 2 percent of students nationwide

Name of Scholarship: Trustee Scholarship
Value: Full tuition
Awards: 100

Loyola Marymount University
Name of Scholarship: Trustee Scholarship
Value: Full tuition + room and board
Awards: 10
Determining Factors: Academic achievement
Minimum Requirements: Minimum 3.6 GPA, SAT math and verbal 650 or ACT 29

Soka University of America
Name of Scholarship: Global Merit Scholarships
Value: Full tuition + transportation + books and supplies + personal expenses + President's Scholars Medallion at commencement + campus parking + annual book allowance
Minimum Requirements: Subject to a continued GPA of 3.0 or higher

California Institute of Technology (Caltech)
Name of Scholarship: Stamps Leadership Scholarship
Value: Full tuition
Minimum Requirements: Nomination, Must apply via non-binding Early Action

University of California, Los Angeles
Name of Scholarship: Stamps Leadership Scholarship
Value: Up to full tuition + enrichment funds of up to $12,000
Awards: 5 national awards, 5 for California residents
Determining Factors: Leadership, scholarship, community service, innovation
Minimum Requirements: Nomination

Delaware

University of Delaware
Name of Scholarship: Eugene DuPont Memorial Scholars
Value: Full tuition + room and board + $375 per semester for textbooks + $2,500 enrichment activities

District of Columbia

American University
Name of Scholarship: Frederick Douglass Scholars Program
Value: Full tuition + fees + room and board + books
Determining Factors: "Preference will be given to first-generation students as well as those committed to working in communities of color in the United States. " Most recipients have at least a 3.2 GPA (unweighted) or 3.4 GPA (weighted) and 1150 SAT (CR+M) or 25 ACT.

Catholic University of America
Name of Scholarship: Archdiocesan Scholarship
Value: Full tuition
Awards: 5
Determining Factors: Academic merit
Minimum Requirements: Minimum 3.8 GPA, 1450 SAT (CR+M) or 32 ACT, top 10% class rank

The George Washington University
Name of Scholarship: Presidential Academic Scholarship
Value: Full tuition

Howard University
Name of Scholarship: Presidential Scholarship
Value: Full tuition + fees + room and board + $950 book voucher + laptop
Determining Factors: Academic achievement
Minimum Requirements: Minimum 3.75 GPA and 1500-1600 SAT (CR+M) or 34-36 ACT

Name of Scholarship: Founders Scholarship
Value: Full tuition+ fees + room and board + $500 book

voucher
Determining Factors: Academic achievement
Minimum Requirements: Minimum 3.5 GPA and 1400-1490 SAT (CR+M) or 32-33 ACT

Name of Scholarship: Capstone Scholarship
Value: Full tuition + fees + room
Determining Factors: Academic achievement
Minimum Requirements: Minimum GPA 3.25 and 1300-1390 SAT (CR+M) or 29-31 ACT

Name of Scholarship: Legacy Scholarship
Value: Tuition + fees
Determining Factors: Academic achievement
Minimum Requirements: Minimum 3.0 GPA (or rank of 1 or 2 in class) and SAT 1170-1290 (CR+M) or 26-28 ACT

Florida

University of Miami
Name of Scholarship: Hammond Scholarship
Value: Full tuition
Determining Factors: Academic excellence, a commitment to personal goals, aspirations of continuing education at the graduate level

Name of Scholarship: Singer Scholarship
Value: Full tuition
Determining Factors: Exceptional qualities and academic achievement

Name of Scholarship: Stamps Foundation Scholarship
Value: Full tuition + fees + room and board + textbooks +

enrichment stipend of $12,000 + leadership programs

Determining Factors: Exceptional qualities and academic achievement

Minimum Requirements: Must apply early decision or early action

Florida A&M

Name of Scholarship: Distinguished Scholar Award

Value: Full tuition + fees + $2,000 stipend for room and board

Determining Factors: 1800 SAT or 27 ACT and a GPA or 3.5 or above

Rollins College

Name of Scholarship: Alfond Scholarship

Value: Full tuition

Awards: 10

Determining Factors: Overall academic record

Minimum Requirements: Most winners have at least a 3.6 GPA and a minimum of 1420 SAT (CR+M) or 32 ACT.

Stevenson University

Name of Scholarship: Presidential Fellowship

Value: Full Tuition Scholarship + $3,000 stipend

Determining Factors: Commitment to academic excellence, proven leadership in school-based activities, community service, and/or athletics

Minimum Requirements: Must apply by November 1st

Barry University

Name of Scholarship: Stamps Leadership Scholarship

Value: Tuition + room and board + $6,000 for study abroad or extraordinary learning experiences + faculty

advisor + leadership opportunities
Determining Factors: Academics, leadership, and community service
Minimum Requirements: Minimum 3.5 GPA

<u>Georgia</u>

Agnes Scott College
Name of Scholarship: Marvin B. Perry Presidential Scholarship
Value: Full tuition + room and board
Determining Factors: Academics, leadership, character, and personal achievement

Emory University
Name of Scholarship: Emory Scholars
Value: Up to full tuition + enrichment stipends
Determining Factors: Academic achievement and extracurricular engagement
Minimum Requirements: Application deadline November 15th

Georgia Institute of Technology
Name of Scholarship: Presidential Scholars
Value: Full tuition + room and board
Determining Factors: Scholarship, leadership, progress, and service

Minimum Requirements: Must apply by October 15th

Name of Scholarship: Stamps Leadership Scholarship
Value: Full tuition + $4,000 for public service internship or research + study abroad or international experience funds up to $8,000

Awards: 5-6 national awards, 5-6 awards for Georgia residents
Determining Factors: Academics, personal achievements, and leadership

University of Georgia
Name of Scholarship: Foundation Fellowship and Bernard Ramsey Honors Scholarship
Value: Full tuition
Determining Factors: Academic achievement, intellectual drive, curiosity, record of leadership and service, intellectual and cultural diversity
Minimum Requirements: Submit application by November 3rd, at least a 3.8 GPA, and a minimum of 2100 SAT or 31 ACT

Name of Scholarship: Stamps Leadership Scholarship
Value: Full tuition + $3,000 travel-study grant
Determining Factors: Overall achievement and leadership
Minimum Requirements: Must apply by mid-November

Oglethorpe University
Name of Scholarship: Jennett Scholars Program
Value: Full tuition + stipend for summer study abroad + eligible for research stipend
Awards: 5
Determining Factors: Academic achievement and extracurricular/community involvement
Minimum Requirements: Must attend Scholarship Weekend

Mercer University
Name of Scholarship: Stamps Leadership Scholarship

Value: Full tuition + fees + room and board + $1,600 for books + iPad + $4,000 for enrichment activities
Awards: 10
Determining Factors: Leadership, perseverance, scholarship, service to humankind and innovation
Minimum Requirements: Must submit application by November 1st

Morehouse College
Name of Scholarship: Stamps Leadership Scholarship
Value: Full tuition + $10,000 enrichment activities
Awards: 5
Determining Factors: Overall achievement and leadership
Minimum Requirements: Minimum 3.7 GPA and must apply by November 1st

Hawaii

University of Hawaii
Name of Scholarship: Regents' Scholarship
Value: full tuition plus $4,000 per year and one time $2,000 travel grant
Awards: 20
Determining Factors: Academic and extracurricular achievement
Minimum Requirements: Minimum 3.5 GPA and 29 ACT or 1950 SAT

Iowa

Cornell College
Name of Scholarship: King Scholarship

Value: Full tuition
Number of Awards: 3-5
Determining Factors: Academic Achievement
Minimum Requirements: Must be in top 5% of admitted students

Drake University
Name of Scholarship: National Alumni Scholarship and George A. Carpenter Scholarship
Value: Full tuition + fees + room and board
Awards: 16
Determining Factors: Scholastic achievement, extracurricular and community activities, leadership, communication skills, and potential for contributing to the academic and extracurricular life
Minimum Requirements: ACT 31 or SAT 1380/1400 (CR +M) and top 5% of class or minimum 3.8 GPA. Students must submit their application by December 1st.

Morningside College
Name of Scholarship: Trustee Scholarship
Value: Full tuition
Determining Factors: 3.9 GPA or above and 31 ACT minimum

Illinois

Knox College
Name of Scholarship: Presidential Scholarship
Value: Full tuition
Awards: 5

Illinois Institute of Technology
Name of Scholarship: Duchossois Leadership Scholars
Value: Full tuition
Minimum Requirements: none

Name of Scholarship: Camras Scholars Program
Value: Full tuition + room and board + paid summer experiences
Determining Factors: Academics, leadership, extracurricular activities, communication skills, positive personality, capacity for original through, sense of caring
Minimum Requirements: Minimum 3.5 GPA, ACT/SAT scores in the top 10% nationally

University of Chicago
Name of Scholarship: Stamps Leadership Scholarship
Value: Full tuition, room and board, $10,000 enrichment funds
Determining Factors: Overall achievement and leadership

University of Illinois – Urbana Champaign
Name of Scholarship: Stamps Leadership Scholarship
Value: Full tuition + $12,000 for enrichment activities
Awards: up to 5
Determining Factors: Leadership, overcoming obstacles, scholarship, service and innovation

Indiana

Indiana University
Name of Scholarship: The Wells Scholarship Program
Value: Full tuition + fees + living stipend
Awards: 18-22

Determining Factors: Academic achievement, leadership, extracurricular activities, community involvement, and character

Minimum Requirements: Most nominees score 1400 or above on SAT (CR+M) or 32 on ACT have 3.9 GPA or higher, and graduate within the top 5% of their class. Scholars must be nominated by their school or the IUB admissions office.

Purdue University
Name of Scholarship: Stamps Leadership Scholarship
Value: Full tuition + $10,000 enrichment funds
Determining Factors: Academics, leadership, extracurricular activities, and personal background and experiences
Minimum Requirements: Submit application by November 1st

University of Notre Dame
Name of Scholarship: Stamps Leadership Scholarship
Value: Full tuition + $12,000 enrichment funds + faculty and professional mentors
Determining Factors: Leadership, perseverance, scholarship, service, and innovation
Minimum Requirements: Nominated by admissions office

Indiana University, Purdue University Fort Wayne
Name of Scholarship: Chancellor's Distinguished Scholarship
Value: Full tuition
Determining Factors: 2100 SAT or 32 ACT or higher

Kentucky

Centre College
Name of Scholarship: Brown Fellows Program
Value: Full tuition
Number of Awards: 10
Determining Factors: Overall achievement

Name of Scholarship: Grissom Scholarship Program
Value: Full tuition
Number of Awards: 10
Determining Factors: Academic achievement, moral character, and leadership potential

Kentucky State University
Name of Scholarship: Presidential Scholarship
Value: Full tuition + fees + room and board + $600 for books and supplies per semester
Minimum Requirements: Minimum 3.5 GPA and 26 ACT, or SAT 1170 (CR+M)

University of Kentucky
Name of Scholarship: Otis A. Singletary Scholarship
Value: Full tuition, room and board, stipend, iPad, $2,000 summer abroad stipend
Minimum Requirements: 31 ACT or 1360 SAT (CR+M) and minimum unweighted GPA of 3.5

Name of Scholarship: Presidential Scholarship
Value: Full tuition
Minimum Requirements: Minimum 31 ACT or 1360 SAT (CR+M) and minimum 3.5 GPA

University of Louisville

Name of Scholarship: Brown Fellows Program
Value: Full tuition + room and board + allowance for books + up to $5,000 in enrichment funds
Awards: 10
Determining Factors: Academics, well-roundedness, leadership potential
Minimum Requirements: 31 ACT or 1360 SAT (CR+M), minimum 3.5 GPA, non-resident of Kentucky (there are other scholarships for Kentucky residents)

Louisiana

Tulane University

Name of Scholarship: Dean's Honor Scholarship
Value: Full tuition
Awards: 75
Determining Factors: General achievement and a creative project
Minimum Requirements: Must submit application by November 15th via Early Action

Name of Scholarship: Paul Tulane Scholarship
Value: Full tuition
Awards: 50
Determining Factors: General Achievement
Minimum Requirements: Must submit application by November 15th via Early Action

Name of Scholarship: Stamps-Tulane Scholarship
Value: Full tuition + enrichment funding
Awards: 5
Determining Factors: Academics, leadership,

perseverance, service and innovation
Minimum Requirements: Must apply for Dean's Honor Scholarship and nominated from that pool

Louisiana State University
Name of Scholarship: Stamps Leadership Scholarship
Value: Full tuition + up to $14,000 enrichment expenses
Minimum Requirements: Selected from students admitted to the honors program, 33 ACT or 1440 SAT (CR+M), and minimum 3.0 GPA

Louisiana Tech University
Name of Scholarship: Presidential Scholarship
Value: Full tuition + fees + room and board
Minimum Requirements: 3.0 GPA or higher and 32 ACT or 1400 SAT (CR+M)

University of Louisiana-Monroe
Name of Scholarship: President's Distinguished Award
Value: Full tuition + fees + $5,000 housing award
Determining Factors: 3.0 GPA or higher; 30-31 ACT or 1320 SAT (CR+M)

Name of Scholarship: President's Distinguished Award - Plus
Value: Full tuition + fees + $5,000 housing award + iPad + $4,500 study abroad stipend
Determining Factors: Minimum 3.75 GPA; 32-36 ACT or 1410 SAT (CR+M)

Maryland

University of Maryland – College Park
Name of Scholarship: Banneker/Key Scholarship

Value: Up to full tuition + room and board + book allowance
Awards: 150
Determining Factors: Academics, leadership
Minimum Requirements: Must be admitted to the Honors College

Name of Scholarship: Stamps Leadership Scholarship
Value: Tuition + room and board + book allowance + up to $5,000 enrichment funds
Awards: 2-3
Determining Factors: Academic leadership
Minimum Requirements: Must be admitted to the Honors College, admitted through the same pool as Banneker/ Key Scholarship

Stevenson University
Name of Scholarship: Presidential Fellowship
Value: Full tuition + $3,000 for faculty-led trip
Determining Factors: Commitment to academic excellence, proven leadership in school-based activities, community service, and/or athletics
Minimum Requirements: Must complete application by November 1st

Massachusetts

Boston College
Name of Scholarship: Presidential Scholars Program
Value: Full tuition
Awards: 15
Determining Factors: Academic record, community service, and leadership

Minimum Requirements: Apply Early Action by November 1st

Boston University
Name of Scholarship: Trustee Scholarship
Value: Full Tuition + fees
Awards: 20
Determining Factors: Academics, service, and extracurricular activities
Minimum Requirements: Apply before December 1st, nomination from high school

Northeastern University
Name of Scholarship: University Scholars
Value: Full tuition
Awards: 120
Determining Factors: Academic achievement, creativity, energy, ideas, ambition to innovate, curiosity, entrepreneurial spirit, vision, confidence, maturity, resourcefulness, passion to make a positive difference, and strong character

Michigan

Michigan State University
Name of Scholarship: Alumni Distinguished Scholarship
Value: Full tuition + fees + room and board + $1,000 stipend annually
Awards: 15
Determining Factors: Academic performance and participation in the MSU Alumni Distinguished Scholarship competition
Minimum Requirements: Must apply by November 1st

and complete an examination

Name of Scholarship: Distinguished Freshman Scholarship
Value: Full tuition + fees
Awards: 20
Determining Factors: Academic Performance and participation in the MSU Alumni Distinguished Scholarship competition
Minimum Requirements: Must apply by November 1st and complete an examination

Mississippi

University of Mississippi
Name of Scholarship: Stamps Leadership Scholarship
Value: Full tuition + $12,000 enrichment stipend
Determining Factors: Academic achievement, leadership, and service

Missouri

Saint Louis University
Name of Scholarship: Presidential Scholarship
Value: Full tuition + up to $1,200 in enrichment funding
Minimum Requirements: Minimum 3.85 GPA and 30 ACT or 1330 SAT (CR+M)

Washington University in St. Louis
Name of Scholarship: John B. Ervin's Scholar Program
Value: Full tuition + $2,500 stipend annually
Determining Factors: "Applicants should excel academically, challenge themselves, demonstrate initiative and leadership in their communities, bring diverse groups

together, commit to community service, serve historically underprivileged populations, and/or persevere through challenging circumstances."

Name of Scholarship: Annika Rodriguez Scholars Program
Value: Full tuition + $2,500 stipend per year
Determining Factors: "Awards are based on academic achievement (strong grades and SAT or ACT scores), a commitment to serving historically underprivileged populations, the ability to bring diverse people together, application answers and essay, and recommendations received as part of the admission application."

Name of Scholarship: Danforth Scholars Program
Value: Full tuition
Determining Factors: "In addition to outstanding academic performance, the committee in interested in activities that illustrate the candidate's exceptional commitment to community service, high moral character, and similar qualities that exemplify the Danforths' legacy at Washington University. The selection committee finds it helpful to learn of specific examples of leadership, academic, and personal achievements that set this student apart from his or her peers."
Minimum Requirements: Must be nominated by person with extensive knowledge of student

Name of Scholarship: Stamps Leadership Scholarship
Value: Full tuition + fees + room and board + supplies + $10,000 enrichment fund
Determining Factors: Academic achievement, leadership, perseverance, scholarship, service and innovation

New Jersey

Stevens Institute of Technology
Name of Scholarship: The Ann P. Neupauer Scholarship
Value: Full tuition
Awards: 30

New York

University of Buffalo
Name of Scholarship: Presidential Scholarship
Value: Full tuition + fees + housing + board and books
Minimum Requirements: Unweighted high school average of 95 and SAT 1470 (CR+M) or ACT score of 33

Fordham University
Name of Scholarship: Presidential Scholarship
Value: Full Tuition + room
Awards: 20
Determining Factors: Academic achievement in high school, test scores, and personal characteristics

Syracuse University
Name of Scholarship: Coronat Scholars
Value: Full tuition + one paid study abroad trip + funding for summer experience + admission to honors program
Determining Factors: Academic achievement, leadership, and service activities

University of Rochester
Name of Scholarship: Renaissance and Global Scholarships

Value: Full tuition + individual mentoring
Awards: 20
Determining Factors: Academic curiosity/excellence and social awareness
and involvement

St. Lawrence University
Name of Scholarship: Trustee Scholarship
Value: Full tuition
Determining Factors: Academic excellence, character and leadership

SUNY Alfred College
Name of Scholarship: Distinguished Scholars Program: Excellence in Education Scholarship
Value: Full tuition + room and board
Determining Factors: GPA of 94 or better through junior year; at least a 1250 (CR+M) or 28 ACT

Hobart and William Smith Colleges
Name of Scholarship: Hersh Scholarships
Number of Awards: 2
Amount: Full tuition + fees
Determining Factors: Academic excellence, extracurricular involvement, and community service

Name of Scholarship: Wood Scholarship
Number of Awards: 1
Amount: Full tuition
Determining Factors: Awarded to the most academically outstanding student

Davidson College
Name of Scholarship: John Montgomery Belk Scholarship
Value: Full tuition + $6,000 for summer experiences
Awards: 8
Determining Factors: Academic achievement, character, leadership, and service
Minimum Requirements: School nomination

Duke University
Name of Scholarship: Robertson Scholars
Value: Full tuition + fees + room and board + funding for up to three summer experiences
Determining Factors: Purposeful leadership, intellectual curiosity, strength of character, and collaborative spirit

University of North Carolina – Chapel Hill
Name of Scholarship: Morehead-Cain Scholars
Value: Full tuition + room and board + books + laptop + funding for research and summer opportunities
Minimum Requirements: All students from Canada, Great Britain, and North Carolina can apply. All other students must come from a designated nomination school or have your school register to become a nomination school. You can find a list of current nominating schools here: http://www.moreheadcain.org/nominating-schools/

Name of Scholarship: Robertson Scholars
Value: Full tuition + fees + room and board + funding for up to three summer experiences
Determining Factors: Purposeful leadership, intellectual curiosity, strength of character, and collaborative spirit

North Carolina State University
Name of Scholarship: Park Scholarship
Value: Full tuition + fees + room and board + books and supplies + travel + laptop + personal expenses + admission to University Scholars Program
Determining Factors: "Academic merit, exemplary character, exceptional potential for leadership, and the sense of promise that they may one day make contributions of enduring importance to the betterment of the human condition"
Minimum Requirements: Endorsement by school or filled out self-endorsement form

Wake Forest University
Name of Scholarship: Nancy Susan Reynolds Scholarship
Value: All expenses associated with attending college + stipend
Determining Factors: Scholarship, achievement, and personal interviews

Name of Scholarship: Stamps Leadership Scholarship
Value: Full tuition + enrichment stipend
Awards: 5
Determining Factors: Educational achievements, academic motivation, maturity and character

University of North Carolina – Charlotte
Name of Scholarship: Levine Scholars Program
Value: Full tuition + room and board + fees + laptop + summer experience funding + study abroad + $8,000 grant to implement a service project + membership to Honors College

Determining Factors: Scholarship, ethical leadership, and civic engagement

North Carolina A&T State University
Name of Scholarship: National Alumni Association Scholarship
Value: Full tuition + fees + room and board + books
Determining Factors: Academic talent and ability
Minimum Requirements: Minimum qualifications include having a 3.0 or higher high school GPA and a 1000 or higher SAT (CR+M) or 22 ACT score.

Name of Scholarship: Lewis and Elizabeth Dowdy Scholarship
Value: full tuition, fees, room and board
Minimum Requirements: 3.75 or higher GPA and a 1200 SAT (CR+M) or 26 ACT score

Salem College
Name of Scholarship: Robert E. Elberson Scholarship
Value: Full tuition + room and board + semester of study abroad in England

Name of Scholarship: Chatham/Davis/Weyand/Womble/ Whitaker Scholarships
Value: Full tuition
Awards: 10-15
Determining Factors: Academic performance, evidence of leadership, responsibility, concern for others, initiative, motivation, creativity, resourcefulness, and vigor

Ohio

Miami University
Name of Scholarship: University Merit Scholarship
Value: Up to full tuition
Determining Factors: Academic achievement and holistic review of application
Minimum Requirements: 32 ACT or 1400 SAT (CR+M), 3.5 GPA

Name of Scholarship: Stamps Leadership Scholarship
Value: Full tuition + fees + room and board + textbooks + $12,000 enrichment funds

Ohio State University
Name of Scholarship: Eminence Scholarship
Value: Full tuition + fees + room and board + books and supplies + $3,000 enrichment
Determining Factors: Academic achievement, contribution to school and local community, and leadership
Minimum Requirements: Recipients typically rank in the top three percent of their graduating classes and have a 34 ACT or 1520 SAT (CR+M)

Denison University
Name of Scholarship: Mary Carr Endowed Scholarship, Dr. Betty Lovelace Scholarship, and Dr. Desmond Hamlet Scholarship
Value: Full tuition
Determining Factors: Academic achievement, outstanding leadership and personal merit

Hiram College

Name of Scholarship: Trustee Scholarship
Value: Full tuition
Determining Factors: Academic achievement
Minimum Requirements: GPA 3.8 and ACT 28 or SAT 1260 (CR+M)

Oberlin College

Name of Scholarship: Stamps Leadership Scholarship
Value: Full tuition + fees + $5,000 enrichment funding
Determining Factors: Excellence in academic and/or musical talent

Oregon

Lewis and Clark College

Name of Scholarship: Barbara Hirschi Neely Scholarship
Value: Full tuition + fees + $2,000 stipend
Determining Factors: Academic achievement and distinctive personal accomplishment. "Special preference is given to students committed to studying the sciences, or students with an unusually keen interest in intercultural and international issues"

Pennsylvania

Arcadia University

Name of Scholarship: President's Scholarship
Value: Full tuition
Determining Factors: Academic excellence, outstanding leadership and community and volunteer service

University of Pittsburgh
Name of Scholarship: University Academic Scholarship
Value: Up to full tuition
Determining Factors: Academic achievement is the primary factor. Activities outside of the classroom such as leadership positions, athletics, community service, etc. are reviewed as a secondary consideration.
Minimum Requirements: Most recipients have a minimum SAT I score of 1450 (CR+M) or 33 ACT composite score, an 'A' average, and a top 5% class rank

Elizabethtown College
Name of Scholarship: Stamps Leadership Scholarship
Value: Full tuition + $4,000 enrichment funds + personal mentor
Determining Factors: Leadership, perseverance, scholarship, service, and innovation

Temple University
Name of Scholarship: President's Scholars
Value: Full tuition + three $4,000 educational enhancement stipends for study abroad, research, internships, or summer academic activities
Determining Factors: 32 ACT or 1400 SAT (CR+M); 3.75 GPA or above

Rhode Island

Providence College
Name of Scholarship: Liberal Arts Honors Scholarship
Value: Up to full tuition (though most offers are between 40-60% of tuition)
Determining Factors: Academic achievement is primary consideration but will also look at extracurricular

activities and personal accomplishments

South Carolina

Clemson University
Name of Scholarship: National Scholars
Value: Full tuition
Awards: 40
Determining Factors: Outstanding academic achievement (average scholar achieved 1500 SAT [CR+M] or 34 ACT and was ranked in top 1% of class), leadership, service, and extracurricular involvement

Furman University
Name of Scholarship: Herman W. Lay Scholarship
Value: Full tuition + fees + room and board
Awards: 4
Determining Factors: Academic Achievement (most recipients have at least a 1400 SAT [CR+ M] or 32 ACT), extracurricular involvement, and personal achievement

Name of Scholarship: James B. Duke Scholarship
Value: Full tuition
Awards: 10
Determining Factors: Awards (most recipients have at least a 1400 SAT [CR+M) or 32 ACT), extracurricular involvement, and personal achievement

Wofford College
Name of Scholarship: The Richardson Family Scholarship
Value: Full tuition + fees + room and board + laptop + summer internships plus one overseas experience + January experience

Determining Factors: Leadership, academic achievement and character
Minimum Requirements: Nomination by school. Top 10 percent of the class and combined score of 1250 (CR+M) on the PSAT or SAT or a 28 on the ACT

<u>Tennessee</u>

Belmont University
Nashville, TN
Name of Scholarship: Presidential Scholarship
Value: Full tuition + fees + room and board + books
Number of Awards: 5
Minimum Requirements: 30 ACT or 1330 SAT (CR+M)

Name of Scholarship: William Randolph Hearst Endowed Scholarship
Value: Full tuition + fees + room and board + books
Number of Awards: 1
Determining Factors: Awarded to a freshman from a diverse background

Rhodes College
Name of Scholarship: Bellingrath Scholarship
Value: Full tuition
Awards: 1
Determining Factors: Academic achievement and personal achievements

Vanderbilt University
Name of Scholarship: Ingram Scholarship
Value: Full tuition + stipends for summer projects
Determining Factors: Commitment to community service, strength of personal character, and leadership potential

Name of Scholarship: Cornelius Vanderbilt Scholarship Program

Value: Full tuition + stipend for one study abroad or research experience

Determining Factors: Academic achievement, intellectual promise, and leadership and contribution outside the classroom

Texas

University of Texas at Austin
Name of Scholarship: 40 Acres Scholarship
Value: Full tuition + fees + books + living stipend + support for enrichment activities

Southern Methodist University
Name of Scholarship: President's Scholar Program
Value: Full tuition + fees + travel expenses and tuition for study abroad
Determining Factors: Academic achievement and a demonstrated commitment to engagement in school and/or community activities
Minimum Requirements: Exceptional achievement on the ACT or SAT, a minimum of 20 high school academic units in a challenging curriculum, including AP/IB and honors courses, two years of a single foreign language, and advanced coursework in math and science, and a high school rank in the top 10 percent of the graduating class

Southwestern University
Name of Scholarship: Brown Scholars
Value: Full tuition

Minimum Requirements: Top 5% of their high school class (or if high school does not rank, have the equivalent of a 3.8 GPA on a 4.0 scale). Students must score at least a 1400 SAT (CR+M) or 31 ACT

Texas Christian University
Name of Scholarship: Chancellor's Scholarship
Value: Full tuition
Awards: 43
Determining Factors: Academic achievement is the primary factor (SAT score average of recipients is 2190. ACT is 33), and leadership accomplishments, service records, and extracurricular activities are also considered.

University of Houston
Name of Scholarship: Tier One Scholarship
Value: Full tuition + fees + two years room and board + stipend for research and study abroad + membership to Honors College + priority registration for classes
Minimum Requirements: Minimum SAT of 1300 (CR +M) or 29 ACT and must rank in the top 10 percent of high school class

University of Texas at Dallas
Name of Scholarship: The McDermott Scholars Program
Value: Full tuition + fees + $1,200 stipend per month to cover room, board, and living expenses + $1,000 annual book stipend + international experience up to $12,000 + professional development experience up to $3,000 + paid travel home twice a year for domestic students and once a year for international students
Awards: 24
Determining Factors: Based on exceptional academic performance (most recipients have 1400 or higher on the

SAT (CR+M) and a class rank in the top 5% of their high school class; community volunteerism and leadership in school; broad and eclectic interests in science, literature, and the arts; and social skills to interact easily with adults as well as peers.

Utah

Utah State University
Name of Scholarship: Presidential Scholarship and Dean's Scholarship
Value: Full tuition (+ fees for Presidential Scholarship)
Determining Factors: Academic achievement based on grades and scores

Utah Valley University
Name of Scholarship: Presidential Scholarship and Exemplary Scholarship
Value: Full tuition (+ fees for Presidential Scholarship)
Determining Factors: Academic achievement based on grades and scores

Virginia

University of Richmond
Name of Scholarship: Richmond Scholars
Value: Full tuition + $3,000 for enrichment activities + priority course registration + guaranteed housing
Determining Factors: Based on outstanding and engaged scholarship; desire to be at the forefront in the creation and discovery of new knowledge; leadership skills; desire to be a leader in service to society; broad worldview; excitement about learning from people who are different from themselves in a diverse community of scholars;

recognition of the importance of personal integrity and ethical decision making; enthusiastic pursuit of self-improvement; desire to make the most of opportunities presented; and exceptional talent in artistic expression.

University of Virginia
Name of Scholarship: Jefferson Scholarship
Value: Full tuition + fees + room and board+ books + personal expenses

Washington and Lee
Name of Scholarship: Johnson Scholarship
Value: Full tuition + room and board + $7,000 to support summer experiences
Determining Factors: Academic and personal accomplishments, essays, performance at in-person scholarship competition (travel expenses are paid by the university for all finalists)

Wisconsin

Carthage College
Name of Scholarship: Presidential Scholarship
Value: Up to full tuition + room and board

Chapter 25
Full Tuition Scholarships for National Merit Semifinalists and Scholars

One of the best ways to get a full tuition scholarship is by becoming a National Merit Scholar or National Merit Semifinalist. Students are considered automatically when they take their PSAT junior year, and if they are selected for the award, they are eligible for many scholarship opportunities at schools throughout the country.

Below, I've put together a list of colleges that offer full tuition scholarships for finalists (and in some cases semifinalists) that are available to out-of-state as well as in-state students and which are automatically awarded. The automatically awarded part is key; unlike other types of merit scholarships which are fixed in number, these scholarships are automatically granted regardless of how many other finalists and semifinalists apply.

If you have been granted one of these honors, be sure to check out this list.

Alabama

Faulkner University
NMSF Award: Full Tuition

NMF Award: Full tuition + fees + room and board

Oakwood University
NMF Award: Full tuition + room
NMSF Award: Full tuition

Troy University
NMF Award: Full tuition + room and board

University of Alabama
NMSF Award: Full Tuition (NMSF + 3.5 GPA required)
NMF Award: Full tuition (up to 5 years) + 1 year housing + $3,500/year + $2,000 expenses + iPad

University of Alabama, Birmingham
NMF Award: Full Tuition + fees + one year of housing + $3,500 annual stipend + $2,000 summer research or study abroad + iPad

University of Alabama, Huntsville
NMSF Award: Full Tuition + fees + $500/year book stipend
NMF Award: Full Ride

Alaska

University of Alaska, Anchorage
NMF Award: Full tuition + $1,000/yr stipend

Arizona

University of Arizona
NMF Award: Full tuition + ($30,000/year + iPad + $1,500 expenses)

Arkansas

Harding University
NMF/NMSF Award: Full tuition

University of Arkansas, Monticello
NMF Award: Full tuition + fees + room and board stipend

California

Pacific Union College
NMF Award: Full tuition
NMSF Award: Half tuition

Florida

Florida A&M
NMF Award: Full tuition + $2000/year books/stipend + laptop
Note: Must major in Biology, Chemistry, Computer Science, Engineering, Environmental Science, Mathematics, or Physics

Florida College
NMF/NMSF Award: Full tuition

Florida International University
NMF Award: Full tuition + fees + room and board

Lynn University
NMF Award: Full tuition

University of Central Florida
NMF Award: Full tuition + laptop + guaranteed housing

Idaho

University of Idaho
NMF Award: Full tuition + fees + room and board

Indiana

University of Evansville
NMF Award: Full tuition
NMSF Award: $20,000/year (approximately 2/3 tuition)

Kansas

Fort Hays State University
NMF Award: Full tuition + fees + room and board + books
NMSF Award: Full tuition + fees + room and board + books

Wichita State University
NMF Award: $20,000/year for non-residents, $12,000/year residents. These funds can be applied to tuition, room and board, and fees.

Kentucky

University of Kentucky
NMF Award: Full tuition + fees + room and board + $1,000 annual stipend + iPad 2 + $2,000 summer abroad program

Louisiana

Louisiana Tech University
NMF Award: Full tuition + fees + room and board + $5,000 bonus award (laptop, study abroad, or 5th year of study)

Maryland

Washington Adventist University
NMF Award: Full tuition
NMSF Award: 3/4 Tuition

Michigan

Andrews University
NMF Award: Full tuition

Minnesota

University of Minnesota, Morris
NMF Award: Full tuition
NMSF Award: Up to $4,000 over four years

Mississippi

Mississippi State University
NMF Award: Full tuition, fees, books, and room
NSMF Award: Full tuition, fees, and books

University of Mississippi
NMF Award: Full tuition + room
NMSF Award: Full tuition + room

University of Southern Mississippi
NMF Award: Full tuition + fees + room and board + books + $4,000 study abroad stipend
NMSF Award: Full tuition + fees

Nebraska

University of Nebraska
NMF Award: Full tuition + $2,000/year

Nevada

University of Nevada, Las Vegas
NMF Award: Full Tuition + Study Abroad

New Hampshire

Rivier University
NMF Award: Full tuition + room and board

New Jersey

New Jersey Institute of Technology
NMF Award: Full tuition + fees + room and board

New York

Roberts Wesleyan College
NMF Award: Full tuition

North Carolina

North Carolina Central University
NMF/NMSF Award: In-state tuition + room and board +

books + $500/semester stipend + internships + laptop

<u>North Dakota</u>

North Dakota State University
NMF Award: Full tuition

<u>Oklahoma</u>

University of Oklahoma
NMF Award: Full tuition + fees + room and board + stipend

Oklahoma City University
NMF Award: Full tuition

Oklahoma Christian University
NMF Award: Full tuition + fees + room and board

Oklahoma Wesleyan University
NMF Award: Full tuition
NMSF Award: Half tuition

<u>Pennsylvania</u>

Drexel University
NMF Award: Full tuition

<u>Tennessee</u>

Bryan College
NMF/NMSF Award: Full tuition

Lipscomb University
NMF Award: Full tuition + fees (note: 10 students per year also will receive room & board)
NMSF Award: Full tuition

Texas

Abilene Christian University
NMF Award: Full tuition

Baylor University
NMF Award: Full tuition

Lubbock Christian University
NMF Award: Full tuition
NMSF Award: $2,000/year

University of Houston
NMF Award: Full tuition + fees + room and board + $3,000 annual stipend

University of North Texas
NMF Award: Full tuition + fees + room and board + books

University of Texas, Arlington
NMF Award: Full tuition + fees + room

University of Texas, Dallas
NMF Award: Full tuition + fees + $8,000/year stipend + $2,000 study abroad funds

University of Texas, Tyler
NMF Award: Full tuition + fees + room and board +

books
NMSF Award: Full tuition + fees + books

<u>Washington</u>

Washington State University
NMF/NMSF Award: Full tuition

<u>West Virginia</u>

Alderson-Broaddus College
NMF Award: Full tuition

Chapter 26
High Paying Outside Scholarships

The scholarships below represent some of the most generous outside scholarships available awarding anywhere from $10,000 to full tuition for their top prizes. Some of these awards are given to traditionally outstanding students who excel both inside and out of the classroom, but others are more focused awarding students with a specialized talent in the arts, an outstanding essay, or based entirely of one science project or leadership activity. Most of the scholarships can be used at any college of your choosing (although several are restricted to a handful of partner colleges) and most are open to students from around the country and in some cases international students as well. There are many outstanding scholarships not included on this list as well. Although this list is a great launching point, I encourage you to visit some of the websites listed in the Scholarship Resources section to expand your search.

Anne Frank Outstanding Scholarship Award
Amount: $10,000
Description: The award seeks to recognize students who "exemplify the commitment, ideals and courage" that Anne Frank represents.
Determining Factors: Students submit a 1,000-word essay about their contributions to their communities and how Anne Frank has inspired their goals. Applicants are

also asked to submit two letters of recommendation. Applicants are evaluated based on their experience acting as spokespersons for tolerance, their experience acting as peacemakers and bridge builders on a daily basis, and in building or participating in programs that address intolerance, violence prevention, and/or conflict resolution.

Ayn Rand Essay Contests

Amount: up to $20,000

Number of Awards: 410

Description: Designed to inspire and intellectually engage students by having them read and respond to Ayn Rand's works.

Determining Factors: Based on a essay answering one of several question options about Atlas Shrugged or the Fountainhead (there are different prizes awarded for both novels).

Buick Achievers Scholarship Program

Amount: up to $25,000 per year for four years

Number of Awards: 25

Description: The scholarship is designed to reward students who have succeeded in and out of the classroom and who may not be able to attend college without financial assistance.

Determining Factors: Scholarships are awarded based on academic achievement and financial need, participation in leadership and school activities and work experience. Preference is given to students with an interests in the automotive or related industry and to students who plan to major in a STEM field. First-generation college students, minorities, females, military veterans and their dependents are also given preference.

CIA Undergraduate Scholarship Program

Amount: up to $18,000 per year

Description: The scholarship was designed to assist minority and disabled student although the application is open to all students. The program pays students up to $18,000 per year for tuition, fees, books, and supplies. Students are given a benefits package that includes health insurance, life insurance, and retirement. Students are required to work for the CIA during summer breaks (cost of transportation and a housing allowance is provided) and work there for 1.5 times the length of the college sponsorship post-graduation.

Requirements: 1500 SAT (1000 CR+M and 500W), 3.0 minimum GPA, maximum household income of $70,000 (family of up to four) or $80,000 (family of five or more)

Determining Factors: Academic achievement, financial need, letters of recommendation, results of polygraph interview, and medical examination

Coca-Cola Scholarship

Amount: $20,000

Number of Awards: 250

Description: One of the biggest scholarships available in the country awarding general academic achievement and leadership.

Requirements: Minimum 3.0 GPA

Determining Factors: The scholarship is awarded based on academic achievement and students' capacity for leadership and service in their schools and communities as reflected in an initial application, recommendations, and from interviews. Recipients are selected during an all-expenses paid trip for finalists to Coca-Cola's headquarters in Atlanta.

213

Davidson Institute for Talent Development

Amount: $10,000-$50,000

Description: The scholarship awards students who have completed significant work in fields related to one of its focus categories: science, technology, engineering, mathematics, literature, music, philosophy, and outside the box.

Determining Factors: Applications are evaluated by the scope and quality of the work, the level of significance of the work submitted, and the applicant's depth of knowledge and understanding of the work and in the related domain area.

Davis-Putter Scholarship

Amount: up to $10,000 per year

Description: The scholarship awards students with need who are active in the progressive movement championing causes such as racism, sexism, homophobia, economic justice, peace through international solidarity, etc.

Determining Factors: Awarded based on academic achievement, 1,000-word personal statement, two letters of recommendation, and financial need.

The Dell Scholars Program

Amount: $20,000, laptop, and textbook credits

Number of Awards: 300

Requirements: Participate in an approved college readiness program (23 programs are currently approved including AVID, Upward Bound, Aspire, Gear Up, Kipp Academy, Uncommon Schools, and IDEA Academy), have a minimum of 2.4 GPA, and proof of demonstrated need (i.e. students must be eligible to receive a Pell grants).

Determining Factors: Determination to succeed, future goals, ability to communicate hardships, self-motivation, and demonstrated need for financial aid. Financial need is weighted more strongly than academic metrics and students on the lower end of the eligible GPA spectrum are highly encouraged to apply.

Dr. Pepper Tuition Giveaway
Amount: up to $100,000
Number of Awards: 21
Description: Dr. Pepper awards a million dollars a year to help students achieve their dreams.
Determining Factors: Students are asked to submit their "goal" which are put up on the website. Once your goal gets 50 votes, you are asked to submit a video explaining the goal in more detail. Finalists are selected to compete in a football throwing competition to compete for the top prizes awarding up to $100,000. The students whose videos get the most votes are also awarded a $5,000 scholarship.

Duck Brand Duct Tape Stuck on Prom Contest
Amount: $10,000
Number of Awards: up to 21
Requirements: Open to students from all US states and Washington DC except for VT, MD, and CO. Legal residents of all Canadian provinces except for Quebec are also eligible.
Description: Applicants create prom attire out of Duck brand duct tape and submit a picture of their creations for evaluation. Applicants can enter as single applicants or as a couple although only couples can receive the first prize award of $10,000 each.
Determining Factors: Judges select winners based on

workmanship, originality, use of color, accessories, and use of duct tape.

Elks Most Valuable Student Scholarship
Amount: $4,000-$50,000
Number of Awards: 500
Description: The scholarship is designed to award students with need for academic achievement and leadership.
Determining Factors: Awarded based off of grades, test scores, leadership experience in activities, an essay, and financial need.

ExploraVision Science Competition
Amount: up to $10,000
Description: The contest encourages students to explore modern technology.
Determining Factors: Students work in teams to explore a piece of technology in their home, school, or community and write a report about its current uses, history, and future technology that may be developed. Students are also asked to explore scientific breakthroughs that may be necessary to improve the technology in the future and how the technology could both positively and negatively impact society. Entries are judged on creativity, scientific accuracy, communication, and feasibility of vision.

From Failure to Promise Essay Contest
Amount: up to $10,000
Number of Awards: 4
Description: The scholarship seeks in inspire and motivate youth by reading and responding to the book "From Failure to Promise: 360 Degrees," an autobiography of Dr. C. Moorer who transformed himself

from a drop-out to an engineer.

Determining Factors: Students submit a 1,500-word essay in response to one of three questions related to the book. Responses are judged based on originality, quality of research, and effectiveness of presentation.

Gallery Collection Scholarship

Amount: $10,000

Number of Awards: 1

Description: Applicants are asked to create an original greeting card using a photo, artwork, or computer graphics. The winner receives the scholarship and their design will be printed and distributed by a national greeting card company.

Determining Factors: The top 10 finalists are determined by popular vote via Facebook. A panel of judges will select the winner evaluating the finalists by quality of execution, creativity and originality, successful incorporation of design elements, appropriateness for use as a greeting card, attractiveness to corporate and consumer customers, and suitability as a design in a Prudent's Gallery Collection greeting.

Gates Millenium Scholarship

Amount: Covers all unmet need and self-help aid, renewable

Number of Awards: 1,000

Description: The scholarship aims to give outstanding African American, American Indian/Alaska Native, Asia Pacific Islander American, and Hispanic American students the opportunity to gain funds for college.

Requirements: Applicants must have a 3.3 GPA minimum; identify and meet the requirements for one of the minority groups; and meet Federal Pell Grant eligibility criteria.

Determining Factors: Awarded based on academic performance, community service and leadership activities, and demonstrated need.

GE - Reagan Foundation Scholarship Program
Amount: up to $10,000 per year

Description: The program seeks to provide college funds for students who demonstrate "exemplary leadership, drive, integrity, and citizenship."

Requirements: Applicants much have 3.0 minimum GPA and demonstrated financial need.

Determining Factors: Awarded based on demonstrated leadership, drive, integrity, and citizenship at school, in the workplace, and in the community; academic performance; and financial need.

Generation Google Scholarship
Amount: $10,000

Description: The scholarship aims to help students who plan to major in computer science, computer engineering, software engineering or a related field or from underrepresented groups in computer science (women, minorities, individuals with a disability).

Determining Factors: Awarded based on academic performance, two letters of recommendation (at least one from a STEM instructor), extracurricular involvement/ work experience, and responses to six short answer questions.

Google Science Fair
Amount: up to $50,000

Description: A global online science and technology competition open to both individuals and teams. Students submit a project related to one of eleven categories including biology, physics, chemistry, computer science and mathematics, energy and space, food science, electricity and electronics, inventions and innovation, flora and fauna, behavioral and social sciences, and Earth and environmental sciences.

Determining Factors: Projects will be assessed by a judging panel who will consider the summary of the project, proposal, method, testing and redesign, and conclusion/report. Finalists will be flown to Google's headquarters to present the project and answer questions in front of a panel of judges in order for the winners to be determined.

Horatio Alger Scholarship Award

Amount: $22,000

Number of Awards: 106

Description: The scholarship recognizes students who have faced and overcome great obstacles and who demonstrate a commitment to use their college degree in service to others.

Requirements: Applicants must demonstrate critical financial need ($55,000 or lower in adjusted gross family income) and have a 2.0 GPA or higher.

Determining Factors: Involvement in extracurricular and community service activities, proof of adversity faced and overcome, and answers to four short essay questions.

Image Cut Games Competition

Amount: up to $50,000

Number of Awards: 3

Description: The competition seeks to honor the most fun and innovative games built with Microsoft tools and technology.

Determining Factors: Students work in teams to create a video game that can be played on Microsoft technology. Entries are judged based on concept, fun, execution, and feasibility.

Intel Science Talent Search

Amount: up to $150,000

Number of Awards: 300

Description: The scholarship awards students who have done original scientific research. Applicants submit a research report which is evaluated by Ph.D scientists, engineers, and mathematicians.

Determining Factors: The scientific research and research report are the primary considerations although general academic achievement as reflected in grades, test scores, and recommendations is also considered.

Jack Kent Cooke Foundation College Scholarship Program

Amount: up to $40,000 per year

Number of Awards: 30-40 students

Description: The scholarship aims to help high-achieving students with financial need pay for college.

Requirements: Applicants must have a 3.5 minimum GPA, 1200 SAT (Critical Reading + Math) or 26 ACT, and family income not exceeding $95,000.

Determining Factors: Recipients are selected based on academic performance and ability, financial need, persistence, a desire to help others and leadership. Applicants submit grades, test scores, essays, letters of recommendation, and information about family finances.

Jack Kent Cooke Young Artist Award

Amount: up to $10,000

Number of Awards: 20

Description: The award is designed to help exceptional young musicians with financial need pay for college.

Determining Factors: Awarded based on exceptional musical achievement, unmet financial need, solid academic achievement, and strength of character.

Jackie Robinson Foundation Scholarship

Amount: up to $24,000 over four years

Number of Awards: 40-60

Description: The scholarship provides college funds to minority high school students who show leadership potential and demonstrate financial need.

Determining Factors: Awarded based on general academic achievement (grades and SAT/ACT scores), financial need, and answers to four essay questions.

National Beta Club Scholarship

Amount: up to $15,000

Number of Awards: 275

Description: Given to outstanding high school students who have the potential to become leaders.

Requirements: Must be a member of the Beta Club as of June 30th before senior year.

Determining Factors: Awarded based on academic excellence, demonstrated leadership, commendable character, community service, essays, letters of recommendation, and involvement in National Beta Club activities.

National Honor Society Scholarship Program

Amount: $1,000-$13,000

Number of Awards: 200

Description: Awarded to outstanding students who are members of the National Honor Society.
Determining Factors: Selection based on service, leadership experience, character, scholarship, and answer to short essay question.

National Peace Essay Contest
Amount: up to $10,000
Number of Awards: 56
Description: The contest seeks to promote discussion about peace and conflict resolution today and in the future.
Determining Factors: Based on answers to a 1,500 word essay responding to an annual topic related to peace.

Point Foundation Scholarship Program
Amount: up to $10,000
Description: The scholarship seeks to nurture the next generation of LGBTQ leaders by supporting scholars involved in the LGBTQ community in achieving their full academic and leadership potential.
Determining Factors: Awarded based on academic performance, proven leadership, desire to make a difference in the world, professional experience, financial need, marginalization, personal and future goals, and involvement in the LGBTQ community.

Proton OnSite Scholarship and Innovation Program
Amount: up to $100,000 awarded over four years
Number of Awards: 1
Description: Awarded to high school seniors who can find new and creative ways to generate and/or use hydrogen power by using renewable and sustainable energy sources.

Requirements: 3.0 minimum GPA

Determining Factors: Based on leadership, work ethic, and community involvement; ability and promise of the idea; thoroughness and presentation of the idea; and strength of recommendations, essay questions, and video essay.

QuestBridge National College Match

Amount: up to full tuition

Number of Awards: 440 in 2013 (varies by year)

Description: QuestBridge helps outstanding low-income high school students gain admission to some of the nation's most selective colleges and universities. QuestBridge partners with 35 colleges including many of the most competitive universities and liberal arts colleges in the country.

Determining Factors: Awarded based on academic achievement, financial qualifications, and personal circumstances.

Ron Brown Scholar Program

Amount: $40,000 (awarded in $10,000 increments for four years)

Description: Awarded to community minded and academically outstanding African American students who have demonstrated an interest in public service, community engagement, business entrepreneurship, and global citizenship.

Requirements: Recipients must be black/African American, must excel academically, exhibit leadership potential, participate in community service activities, and demonstrate financial need.

Determining Factors: Based on transcripts, letters of recommendation, SAT and/or ACT scores, two 500-word essays, leadership, activities, community service, and financial need.

Ronald McDonald House Charities Scholarship
Amount: $1,000 to $100,000 over four years
Description: The scholarship is designed to provide funds to students with financial need who have demonstrated academic achievement and who have been leaders in their communities.
Requirements: Students must live in an area covered by a RMHC, 2.7 GPA minimum.
Determining Factors: Based on scholastic performance, involvement in the community, financial need, and essay content.

Siemens Math, Science, and Technology Award Scholarships
Amount: $1,000-$100,000
Description: The competition is designed to recognize students with talents related to math, science, and technology and who have engaged in scientific research. Applicants submit a research report relating to scientific research they have engaged in.
Determining Factors: Reports are judged based off of scientific importance, creativity, field knowledge, comprehensiveness, interpretation, literature review, potential for future work, clarity, presentation and teamwork (in the case of team submissions).

Teens Drive Smart Video Contest
Amount: $5,000-$20,000
Number of Awards: 3
Description: Applicants submit an original video about safe driving.

Determining Factors: Based on effectiveness in communicating the concept and message (50%); the degree to which the video motivates people to be more safety-conscious (25%); the creativity in delivering the concept and message (25%).

TheDream.US Scholarship Program
Amount: up to $25,000
Description: Awarded to highly motivated students with financial need. Students must pursue a degree at one of the program's partner colleges.
Requirements: Recipients must be eligible for in-state tuition at one of the public partner colleges (in Arizona, California, Florida, Illinois, New York, Texas, Virginia, and Washington DC) or be interested in attending one of the private or nationwide partner colleges, demonstrate financial need, be first-time college students, and have a 2.5 minimum GPA.
Determining Factors: Based on academic achievement as reflected in your grades, standardized test scores, and participation in advanced courses; extracurricular activities including volunteer work and community services; financial need; academic potential and motivation to succeed in college and life as assessed through essays and letter of recommendation.

Vegetarian Resource Group Scholarship
Amount: up to $10,000
Number of Awards: 4
Description: Scholarships awarded to vegetarian high school students who promote vegetarianism in their school or community.
Determining Factors: Applicants evaluated based on an essay about vegetarianism and their future goals.

Voice of Democracy Scholarship

Amount: $1,000-$30,000

Description: The scholarship is designed to give students the opportunity to express their democratic ideas and principles by recording a 3-5 minute speech related to an annual theme.

Determining Factors: Students are evaluated based on the treatment of the theme, clear expression and organization of ideas, and the delivery of the speech.

The WyzAnt College Scholarship

Amount: up to $10,000

Number of Awards: 3

Description: The award seeks to promote education.

Determining Factors: Students submit a 300-word essay describing one way that education has empowered them. Finalists are selected by popular vote and the winner is selected through a review by WyzAnt tutors.

Young American Creative Patriotic Art Award

Amount: up to $10,000

Number of Awards: 5

Description: Sponsored by the Ladies Auxiliary, this scholarship encourages young artists to produce patriotic works.

Determining Factors: Students submit a piece of patriotic artwork using water color, pencil, pastel, charcoal, tempera, crayon, acrylic, pen-and-ink, or oil. Entries are judged based on originality of concept, presentation, patriotism expressed, clarity of ideas, uniqueness, design technique, and total impact of work.

Chapter 27
Additional Outside Scholarships

There are scholarships available to all types of students. Some are based off of academic accomplishments or community involvement. Others are based on an essay or original arts submission. Others select winners through a lottery giving every applicant a random chance. Below you will find a sampling of some lower value scholarships (under $10,000) that are available. While none of these scholarships alone will likely eliminate your debt, when combined together, these scholarships can end up providing you with substantial funds. All of these scholarships are nationally run and open to students from all (or at least most) states. As you will notice, there is something for everyone. And keep in mind that there are thousands of small scholarship opportunities like this available which you can find with a little bit of research. Looking into local scholarships is especially recommended as they often give away the same amount of money as many national scholarships while being slightly less competitive.

100 Black Men Future Leader Scholarship Program
Amount: $1,000-$2,000
Requirements: Minimum 2.5 GPA, at least 50 hours of community service within the past six months
Description: Awards are based primarily based on leadership experience and a 600-word essay on a topic

related to leadership.

AFA Teens for Alzheimer's Awareness College Scholarship

Amount: up to $5,000

Number of Awards: 10

Determining Factors: Students are asked to submit an autobiography and write a 1,200 to 1,500-word essay that describes how Alzheimer's has changed or impacted your life and what you've learned about yourself, your family, and your community in the face of dealing with Alzheimer's disease.

American Association of Candy Technologists Scholarship

Amount: $5,000

Qualifications: Minimum 3.0 GPA

Description: The scholarship is open to students with a demonstrated interest in confectionery technology through research projects, work, formal study, or other experience and who plan on majoring in food science, chemical science, biological science, or related areas.

American Fire Sprinkler Association Scholarship

Amount: $2,000

Number of Awards: 10

Description: Applicants must the "Fire Sprinkler Essay" and answer a ten-question multiple choice open-book test about the reading. For each question answered correctly, students will be given one entry into a random drawing which will award ten $2,000 awards.

AXA Achievement Community Scholarship

Amount: up to $2,500

Number of Awards: 375

Determining Factors: Applications require students to answer essay questions, list their GPA, work experience, and involvement in school and community activities although primary consideration is given to non-academic achievements. Evaluation is based on ambition and drive, determination to set and reach goals, respect for self, family, and community, and ability to succeed in college. Special consideration is given "to achievements that empower society to mitigate risk thorough education and/or action in areas such as financial, environmental, health, safety and/or emergency-preparedness."

Castle Ink Paperless Scholarship

Amount: $1,000

Number of Awards: 1

Description: The scholarship aims to promote awareness about recycling. You can enter by either posting something about recycling and how you recycle on social media or by making something cool out of recycled materials.

Common Knowledge Scholarship

Amount: up to $2,500

Description: Applicants compete in online competitions where they answer questions on trivia knowledge covering academic subjects as well as pop culture (different competitions have different focuses). Winners are determined on the basis of both time and accuracy.

Courageous Persuaders Video Scholarship Competition

Amount: up to $2,000 (or up to $3,000 for Michigan residents)

Number of Awards: 13

Description: Applicants submit a 30-second commercial aimed at middle schoolers to teach them about the dangers of underage drinking.

Discover Loan Scholarship

Amount: $1,000

Number of Awards: 40

Determining Factors: Winners are selected through a random drawing.

Dupont Challenge Science Essay Competition

Amount: up to $5,000

Determining Factors: Applicants submit a 700- to 1,000-word related to one of four topics: global food access and nutrition, energy and natural resources, environmental sustainability, and innovation. Essays are evaluated based on mechanics and conventions (25%), ideas and content (25%), organization (20%), style and creativity (20%), and voice (10%).

Education Matters $5K Scholarship

Amount: $5,000

Number of Awards: 1

Description: Based on a 250-word response to the question, "What would you say to someone who thinks education doesn't matter, or that college is a waste of time and money?"

Flavor of the Month Scholarship

Amount: $1,500

Number of Awards: 1

Description: Based on a 250-word response to the question, "If you were an ice cream flavor, which would you be and why?"

Frame My Future Scholarship
Amount: $1,000
Number of Awards: 5
Description: Submit an original photograph, collage, poem, drawing, or painting related to the theme "This is how I frame my future."

Gedunk Award for Tolerance
Amount: $1,000
Determining Factors: Students submit an original work of art or writing which considers their role in cultivating tolerance by reflecting upon lessons learned through the Holocaust and other genocides.

Get Up Get Active Scholarship
Amount: $1,000
Number of Awards: 1
Description: Awarded based on a 500-word essay answering a question related to the importance of being active.

Healthy Lifestyle Scholarship
Amount: $5,000
Number of Awards: 1
Determining Factors: Students are evaluated based on their answer to two essay questions, the first about the importance of living a healthy lifestyle while in school and the second related to their career plans, goals, and ambitions.

How do You Make College Cheaper Scholarship
Amount: $500

Description: Create a less than a sentence answer to the question, "How do you make college cheaper?" and posting your response on social media.

Humanist Essay Contest
Amount: $1,000
Determining Factors: Applicants submit an essay related on any topic suitable and appropriate for publication in the *Humanist* magazine. Essays are evaluated based on their originality of thought, sense of emotional engagement, clarity and quality of presentation, amount of research evidenced, and future potential shown by the author.

Illustrators of the Future Contest
Amount: up to $5,000
Number of Awards: 4
Description: Applicants submit three science fiction illustrations in black-and-white or color drawn from their imaginations. Artwork is judged by professional artists.

Kohl's Cares Scholarship
Amount: Up to $9,000
Determining Factors: Applicants must be nominated and determination is made by the information provided by the nominator regarding the student's community service activities. Academic achievement and financial need are not taken into account.

Make Us Laugh Scholarship
Amount: $1,500
Number of Awards: 1
Description: Based on a 250-word response where you describe an incident in your life, funny or embarrassing

(fact or fiction) that will make the judges laugh.

National Make it Yourself Wool Competition

Amount: up to $2,000

Description: Applicants submit a wool garment of their creation which are judged on the basis of quality, creativity, design, presentation, and appropriateness with the contestant's lifestyle.

Poster Contest for High School Students

Amount: up to $1,000

Number of Awards: 8

Description: Applicants submit a poster with an illustration related to the theme "You can make a difference."

Project Yellow Light Scholarship

Amount: up to $5,000

Number of Awards: 3

Determining Factors: Applicants are asked to submit a short video encouraging their friends to avoid distracted driving.

Scholar Athlete Milk Mustache of the Year (SAMMY) Award

Amount: $7,500

Number of Awards: 25

Requirements: At least 3.2 GPA and participation in a high school or club sport.

Description: Applicants must describe how drinking milk has been a part of their life and training regimen in 25 words or fewer.

School Band and Orchestra Magazine Scholarship
Amount: $1,000
Number of Awards: 5
Description: Scholarship is awarded on the basis of an essay answering the question "How does music class prepare you for life?"

SEFA Student Design Contest
Amount: up to $6,000
Number of Awards: 3
Description: Applicants are asked to design a piece of furniture or lab equipment which would enhance the scientific laboratory experience. Entries are judged by industry professionals.

Sophie Major Memorial Duck Calling Contest
Amount: up to $2,000
Number of Awards: 4 awards of varying amounts
Description: Awarded to high school seniors on the basis of performance at a duck calling competition in Arkansas.

STARFLEET Scholarship
Amount: up to $1,000
Number of Awards: 5
Description: Applicants must have been a member of STARFLEET for one year prior to applying for the scholarship. Scholarships are awarded in five categories based on prospective field of study including engineering and technology; medical and veterinarian; aspiring writers and artists; business, language studies, and education; and miscellaneous.

Superpower Scholarship
Amount: $2,500

Number of Awards: 1

Description: Based on a 250-word response to the word, "Which superhero or villain would you want to change places with for a day and why?"

Tall Clubs International Scholarship

Amount: up to $1,000

Requirements: Males must be 6'2" or taller, females 5'10" or taller

Description: Scholarship is awarded on the basis of essay entitled "What Being Tall Means to Me."

Technology Addiction Awareness Scholarship

Amount: $1,000

Number of Awards: 1

Determining Factors: Applicants are asked to submit a 140-character message about technology addiction. The top ten finalists will be asked to submit a 500- to 1,000-word, and the winner is selected from this pool.

Top Ten List Scholarship

Amount: $1,500

Number of Awards: 1

Description: Based on a list you are asked to submit of the top ten reasons you should receive this scholarship.

Writers of the Future Contest

Amount: up to $5,000

Number of Awards: 13

Description: Applicants submit a science fiction or fantasy short story or novelette. Stories are judged by professional writers.

The Zombie Apocalypse Scholarship
Amount: $2,000
Number of Awards: 1
Description: Based on a response (no more than 250 words) detailing with what you would do if your school were overrun by zombies.

Chapter 28
Institutional Art Scholarships
(For art, music, dance, theatre, and debate)

<u>Alabama</u>

Auburn University - Auburn University, AL
Name of Scholarship: Art Scholarships
Amount: up to $1,000
Description: Awarded to students who plan to be art or art history majors.

Huntingdon College - Montgomery, AL
Name of Scholarship: Scarlett and Grey Instrumental Award
Amount: $11,500
Description: Awarded to students who plan on participating in the marching band and concert band.

Name of Scholarship: Scarlett and Grey Award
Amount: $11,000
Description: Awarded to students who plan to participate in marching band, pom squad, or cheerleading.

Name of Scholarship: Judy Marley Montgomery Choir Award
Amount: $11,000
Description: Awarded to students who plan to participate in the Concert Choir.

Alaska

University of Alaska at Anchorage - Anchorage, AK
Name of Scholarship: Muriel Hannah Scholarship in Art
Amount: Minimum $500 annually
Description: Awarded to students who have demonstrated a talent in art.

Name of Scholarship: Excellence in Speech and Debate Scholarship
Amount: Minimum $500 annually
Description: Awarded to students who are or plan to be speech and debate team members and who have demonstrated skill in these areas.

Arizona

Arizona State University - Tempe, AZ
Name of Scholarship: School of Dance, Film, and Theater General Scholarship
Amount: Varies
Description: Awarded to students who plan to study the visual and performing arts including dance, theater and stagecraft, film and video, photography, entertainment, and media management.

Arkansas

Hendrix College - Conway, AR
Name of Scholarship: Performing Arts Scholarship
Amount: $2,000 annually
Description: Awarded to students based on talent in music, theatre, and art (open to non-majors).

California

St. Mary's College of California - Moraga, CA
Name of Scholarship: Brother Cornelius Video Arts Scholarship
Amount: $13,000 annually
Description: Awarded to students with accomplishments related to video production or related media. The recipient must major in Art Practice. Applicants are evaluated on the basis of an essay, letters of recommendation, a DVD or online portfolio of original work, software skills, and any relevant video media arts projects.

Name of Scholarship: Performing Arts Scholarships
Amount: $13,000 annually
Description: Awarded to students with demonstrated excellence in music, dance, and theater.

Colorado

Colorado State University - Fort Collins, CO
Name of Scholarship: Colorado State Music Scholarships
Amount: Varies
Description: Awarded to students with outstanding musical talents. Some of these scholarships require that students major in music or a related area.

University of Northern Colorado - Greeley, CO
Name of Scholarship: School of Art and Design Scholarships
Amount: Varies
Description: Awarded to students with outstanding art

portfolios who plan to declare an art major.

Connecticut

University of Hartford - West Hartford, CT
Name of Scholarship: Artistic Merit Scholarship
Amount: up to $15,000
Description: Awarded to students enrolled in the Hartford Art School based on a review of a portfolio review and academic achievement.

Name of Scholarship: Hartt Performing Arts Scholarship
Amount: up to full tuition
Description: Awarded to students who plan to enroll in the Hartt School with talents in music, dance, or theatre. Awards are determined based on an audition and academic achievement.

Delaware

University of Delaware - Newark, DE
Name of Scholarship: Music Scholarships
Amount: up to $10,000
Description: Awarded to students who plan to major in music based on an audition.

Florida

University of Miami - Coral Gables, FL
Name of Scholarship: Music Scholarships
Amount: $5,000 annually to full tuition + enrichment stipend
Description: Recipients must demonstrate exceptional music talent and significant academic achievement above

the average profile of the typical student admitted to the university.

Georgia

Berry College - Mount Berry, GA
Name of Scholarship: Performing Arts Scholarships
Amount: Varies
Description: Awarded to exceptional students musicians or theatre students.

Name of Scholarship: Art Scholarship
Amount: Varies
Description: Awarded to students interested in majoring or minoring in Art (studio art, art history, or art education). Recipients are evaluated based on a portfolio evaluation and interview. (studio art and art education) or an art history evaluation (art history).

Name of Scholarship: English-Creative Writing and Nadassy Scholarship
Amount: Varies
Description: Awarded to students interested in majoring in English or creative writing or minoring in writing. Students must demonstrate experience in creative writing by submitting a portfolio including five original pieces in two different genres.

Name of Scholarship: Viking Drum Line Scholarship
Amount: Varies
Description: Awarded to students who have demonstrated significant ability and potential within marching percussion.

Name of Scholarship: Forensics/Speech Scholarship
Amount: Varies
Description: Awarded to students interested in joining and competing with the Berry College Forensics Union.

Emory University - Atlanta, GA
Name of Scholarship: Dean's Music Scholarships
Amount: Half tuition to full tuition
Description: Awarded on the basis of outstanding promise in their applied areas of music and who demonstrate outstanding academic achievement. Recipients must plan to major in music.

Hawaii

Hawaii Pacific University - Honolulu, HI
Name of Scholarship: Music Ensemble Scholarships
Amount: Varies
Description: Awarded to students with exceptional musical talents in instrumental music.

Name of Scholarship: Cheer and Dance Scholarship
Amount: Varies
Description: Awarded to students with exceptional abilities related to cheer and/or dance.

Name of Scholarship: Debate Scholarship
Amount: up to $6,000 annually
Description: Awarded to students who are interested in participating in the HPU debate program.

Idaho

The College of Idaho - Caldwell, ID

Name of Scholarship: Talent-Based Scholarships
Amount: Varies
Description: Awarded to students who display talents in art, debate, music, or theatre (including playwriting and technical theatre).

Illinois

Augustana College - Rock Island, IL
Name of Scholarship: Art Scholarship
Amount: $500-$4,000 annually
Description: Awarded to students upon review of their art portfolios.

Name of Scholarship: Debate Scholarship
Amount: $500-$4,000 annually
Description: Based on proficiency in debate.

Name of Scholarship: Music Scholarship
Amount: up to $4,500 renewable annually
Description: Awarded to musically talented students (including non-majors) based on a music audition.

Name of Scholarship: Carl B. Nelson Music Education Scholarship
Amount: $500 annually
Number of Awards: Five
Description: Awarded to students planning to major in music education

Name of Scholarship: Theatre Scholarships
Amount: $2,500-$16,000 annually
Description: Awarded to exceptional individuals pursuing performance, technical theatre, playwriting or criticism.

Recipients are selected after an on-campus audition or presentation.

Indiana

Indiana University - Bloomington, IN
Name of Scholarship: Music Scholarships
Amount: Varies
Description: Awarded to students who display exceptional musical talent and who plan on enrolling in the Jacobs School of Music.

Bethel College - Mishawaka, IN
Name of Scholarship: Visual Arts, Music, and Theatre Arts
Amount: $2,000-$16,000 renewable annually
Description: Awarded based on outstanding performance or achievement in visual arts, music, or theatre arts.

Iowa

Cornell College - Mount Vernon, IA
Name of Scholarship: Cornell College Art Award
Amount: $1,000-$4,000 renewable annually
Description: Awarded to students with outstanding abilities in arts. Recipients are not required to participate in the art department's courses or activities.

Name of Scholarship: Cornell College Music Award
Amount: $1,000-$10,000 renewable annually
Description: Awarded to students with musical talents regardless of major. Recipients are required to participate in at least one major ensemble in their principal instrument.

Name of Scholarship: Cornell College Music Scholarship
Amount: $17,000-$25,000 renewable annually
Description: Awarded to students who with exceptional musical abilities. Recipients are required to participate in at least one major ensemble, enroll in music lessons, and participate in a music performance seminar. The scholarship is available to students in all majors.

Name of Scholarship: Cornell College Theatre Award
Amount: $1,000-$4,000 renewable annually
Description: Awarded to students with talents in the theatre arts. Recipients are not required to participate in the department's courses or activities.

Morningside College - Sioux City, IA
Name of Scholarship: Talent Awards
Amount: Varies
Description: Awarded to students with exceptional talents in music (instrumental, vocal, or show choir), art, or theatre who plan on participating in related activities in college.

Kansas

Bethel College - North Newton, KS
Name of Scholarship: Fine Arts Awards
Amount: $4,000-$7,000 annually
Description: Awarded to students with talents in art, music, theater, and forensics based on an audition or an evaluation of a portfolio.

Kentucky

Centre College - Danville, KY
Name of Scholarship: Performing Arts Scholarship
Amount: up to $5,000 annually
Number of Awards: up to 40
Description: Awarded to talented musicians, actors, and theater technicians. Recipients are not required to major in these areas but must have an interest in further developing their skills in these areas.

Louisiana

Louisiana Tech University - Ruston, LA
Name of Scholarship: School of Design Scholarship
Amount: Varies
Description: Awarded to students with exceptional talents in the arts (studio art, photography, or communication design).

Maine

University of Maine - Orono, ME
Name of Scholarship: Visual and Performing Arts Scholarship
Amount: $1,000-$2,000 renewable annually
Description: Awarded to students with exceptional abilities in art, music, or theatre. Recipients are determined based on the evaluation of a portfolio or an audition.

Maryland

Goucher College - Baltimore, MD

Name of Scholarship Fine and Performing Arts Scholarships
Amount: $10,000 annually
Description: Awarded to students with a demonstrated interest and abilities in dance, theatre, music, or the visual arts. Finalists are invited to campus for an audition or portfolio review and for an interview.

Massachusetts

Berklee College of Music - Boston, MA
Name of Scholarship: Merit Scholarships
Amount: Varies
Description: Berklee offers a number of scholarship options for students with talents in music and/or composition.

Boston University - Boston, MA
Name of Scholarship: College of Fine Arts Scholarships
Amount: Varies
Description: Available to students who demonstrate exceptional talent in music, theatre, or visual arts.

Lesley College - Cambridge MA
Name of Scholarship: College of Art and Design Presidential Scholarship
Amount: $10,000 annually
Description: Awarded to students with a strong art portfolio and at least a 3.5 GPA or who have an *exceptional* portfolio and a minimum SAT of 1950 (CR+M+W) or 30 ACT.

Name of Scholarship: College of Art and Design Dean's Scholarship

Amount: $9,000 annually

Description: Awarded to students with a strong art portfolio plus a minimum SAT of 1650 (CR+M+W)/ACT 24 or who have an *exceptional* art portfolio and at least a 3.0 GPA.

Name of Scholarship: College of Art and Design Scholarship

Amount: $8,000 annually

Description: Awarded to students with a strong portfolio and at least a 3.0 GPA or higher plus a minimum 1400 SAT (CR+M+W)/20 ACT or an *exceptional* portfolio and at least a 2.7 GPA.

Michigan

Kalamazoo College - Kalamazoo, MI

Name of Scholarship: Enlightened Leadership Award for the Arts

Amount: $5,000 renewable annually

Number of Awards: 20

Description: Awarded to students with exceptional talents and accomplishments in vocal/instrumental music, theatre arts, visual arts, creative writing, or journalism.

Minnesota

St. Olaf College - Northfield, MN

Name of Scholarship: Art Scholarships

Amount: $6,000 annually

Description: Awarded to students to students with exceptional art talent. The scholarship is open to art and non-art majors.

Name of Scholarship: Dance Scholarships
Amount: $4,000-$8,,000 annually
Description: Awarded to students with exceptional dance talent. Recipients are required to participate in a performance-based project and a movement class each year.

Name of Scholarship: Music Scholarships
Amount: $1,500-$11,500 annually
Description: Awarded to students with exceptional music talent. The scholarship is open to music majors and non-majors.

Name of Scholarship: Theater Scholarship
Amount: $6,000 annually
Description: Awarded to students with exceptional theater talent. The scholarship is open to theater majors and non-majors.

Mississippi

Millsaps College - Jackson, MS
Name of Scholarship: Distinguished Merit in Art, Theatre, Art History, and Music
Amount: $1,500 to $15,000 annually
Description: Awarded to students who are interested in majoring in art, theatre, art history, and music. Awards based on a portfolio and an interview (art); an essay, monologue, and interview (theatre); humanities paper, essay, and interview; audition (music).

Missouri

Washington University - St. Louis - St. Louis, MO

Name of Scholarship: Howard Nemerov Writing Scholars Program in Arts & Sciences
Amount: $3,000 renewable annually
Number of Awards: up to 10
Description: Given to entering freshmen who are gifted writers. Grades and scores are also considered in the selection process.

Name of Scholarship: Conway/Proetz Scholarship in Art
Amount: $6,000-full tuition renewable annually
Number of Awards: One full tuition scholarship and up to five $6,000 scholarships
Description: Awarded to students who have demonstrated outstanding artistic and scholastic accomplishments for a career in the visual arts. High school records and SAT/ACT scores are also considered.

Montana

Montana State University - Bozeman, MT
Name of Scholarship: Spring Free Scholarship
Amount: In-state tuition during the spring semester annually
Description: Awarded to students with exceptional musical abilities who plan on majoring in music. Both residents and non-residents are eligible but tuition waiver for the second semester each year is available up to the in-state amount.

Name of Scholarship: School of Music Scholarships
Amount: Varies
Description: Awarded to students with exceptional musical abilities based on an audition. The scholarship is open to all students regardless of major.

Name of Scholarship: Art Scholarship
Amount: $3,000 annually
Description: Awarded to students with talents in the visual arts based on a portfolio review. Students must plan on majoring in the Studio Arts (painting, drawing, ceramics, printmaking, metal-smithing/jewelry and sculpture), Graphic Design, or Art Education.

Nebraska

Hastings College - Hastings, NE
Name of Scholarship: Talent Scholarships
Amount: Varies
Description: Awarded to students with talents in art, cheerleading, dance, media (journalism, radio, television, videography, photography, and website design), music, speech/forensics, and theatre.

Nevada

Sierra Nevada College - Incline Village, NV
Name of Scholarship: Fine Arts Department Scholarships
Amount: $10,000 or $17,000 annually
Description: Awarded to students who participate in specific art shows selected by the SNC Fine Arts Department.

New Hampshire

Franklin Pierce University - Rindge, NH
Name of Scholarship: Robert Alvin Scholarship in Music
Amount: $2,000 renewable annually
Number of Awards: 2

Description: Awarded to students who have an interest in participating in music at Franklin Pierce. Applicants are asked to s submit a performance and training resume, letters of recommendation, and a video or audio recording.

New Jersey

Drew University - Madison, NJ
Name of Scholarship: Presidential Scholarship in the Arts
Amount: $20,000 total ($5,000 per year for four years)
Description: Awarded to students who have demonstrate exceptional talent in art, music, creative writing, dance, or theater arts (including acting, design, and playwriting). Recipients are not required to major in an artistic field but are required to participate in the arts while in college.

New Mexico

University of New Mexico - Albuquerque, NM
Name of Scholarship: Harriet and John D. Robb Scholarship
Amount: Varies
Description: Awarded to an incoming freshman with talents in musical performance or composition. Recipients must plan to major in music.

Name of Scholarship: Nancy and Howard Stump Endowed Scholarship Fund
Amount: Varies
Description: Awarded to an incoming freshman pursuing a degree in instrumental music. The award is based on talent and need.

Hobart and William Smith Colleges - Geneva, NY
Name of Scholarship: Arts Scholarships
Amount: $3,000-$17,000 annually
Description: Awarded by the fine arts faculty in dance, music, creative writing, theatre, architecture, and studio art to students who demonstrate excellence in one of these areas. Applicants do not need to plan on majoring in one of these fields but must intend on continuing to participate in these areas during college.

Ithaca College - Ithaca, NY
Name of Scholarship: Ithaca Premier Talent Scholarship
Amount: up to $16,000 renewable annually
Description: Awarded to students majoring in music and theater.

Manhattan College - Riverdale, NY
Name of Scholarship: Performing Arts Scholarship
Amount: Varies, renewable by semester
Description: Given to students who have demonstrated exceptional ability in instrumental or vocal music. Recipients must plan to enroll in at least two performing arts ensembles.

Name of Scholarship: Quadrangle Scholarship
Amount: $2,500 per semester renewable every semester
Description: Awarded to students who have experience working for their high school's newspaper, yearbook, and literary magazine and want to continue that interest at Manhattan College by working on the student publication *The Quadrangle*.

Skidmore College - Saratoga Springs, NY
Name of Scholarship: Filene Music Scholarship
Amount: $12,000 renewable annually
Number of Awards: up to 4
Description: Awarded to students with exceptional musical talents. Students are not required to major in music.

North Carolina

Salem College - Winston-Salem, NC
Name of Scholarship: Music Scholarship
Amount: $1,000-$16,000
Description: Awarded to incoming students with outstanding musical ability who intend to major or minor in music. Applicants must audition on the campus or in exceptional circumstances, submit a recorded tape. Students are also asked to submit a reference from a music teacher. Applicants are evaluated based on general musicianship, technical proficiency, and level of repertoire. Academic achievement and citizenship are also considered.

Name of Scholarship: John Preston Davis Art Full-Tuition Scholarship
Amount: Full tuition renewable annually
Description: Awarded to students planning to major in Studio Art, Art History, or Design. Students are asked to submit an essay and provide a letter of recommendation from an art teacher. Finalists will be invited to an interview where they are asked to present their art portfolio.

Wake Forest University
Winston-Salem, NC
Name of Scholarship: Presidential Scholarships
Amount: $16,000 renewable annually
Number of Awards: 20
Description: Awarded to students who demonstrate a solid academic background and extraordinary achievement in dance, music, art, theatre, and debate. Students are not required to major in the achievement area but should plan on participating in the activity in college.

Name of Scholarship: The Russell Brantley Scholarship for Writing
Amount: Varies
Description: Awarded to students with exceptional talent in writing.

North Dakota

University of Jamestown - Jamestown, ND
Name of Scholarship: Fine Arts Participation Award
Amount: $500-$2,500 annually
Description: Awarded to students who demonstrate abilities in music, theatre, and art and who plan to participate in these areas during college.

Name of Scholarship: Dance Activity Award
Amount: $2,000
Description: Awarded to students who demonstrate abilities in dance in dance during college.

Name of Scholarship: Music Major Award
Amount: $3,000-$6,500 annually

Description: Awarded to students who demonstrate musical ability and plan to major in music.

Name of Scholarship: The Student Media Scholarship
Amount: $500-$2,500
Description: Awarded to students who have talents in media production and business activities and who plan on participating in media related activities for an organization (including student publications, the campus radio station, among others).

Ohio

The College of Wooster - Wooster, OH
Name of Scholarship: Performing Arts Scholarship
Amount: $2,000-$8,000 annually
Description: Awarded to students on the basis of accomplishment and promise in music, theatre/dance, or Scottish Arts. Students are not required to major in the area in which they receive their scholarships.

Kenyon College - Gambier, OH
Name of Scholarship: Studio Art Scholarships
Amount: $15,000 renewable annually
Description: Awarded based on a demonstrated exemplary ability in studio art. Recipients are expected to take studio art courses each year but are not required to major in studio art.

Name of Scholarship: Music Scholarships
Amount: $15,000 renewable annually
Description: Awarded based on a demonstrated exemplary ability in any instrumental or vocal category in which the Department of Music offers private

instruction. Recipients are not required to major in music but are expected to take private lessons each semester and take at least one music course each semester.

Name of Scholarship: Kenyon Writing Award
Amount: $15,000 renewable annually
Description: Awarded based on demonstrated writing ability. The winner is selected based on an evaluation of the Common Application essay as well as any other submitted materials.

Name of Scholarship: S. Georgia Nugent Award in Creative Writing
Amount: $15,000 renewable annually
Description: Awarded based on demonstrated creative writing ability. The winner is selected based on an evaluation of the Common Application as well as any other submitted materials.

Oberlin College - Oberlin, OH
Name of Scholarship: Conservatory Dean's Scholarship
Amount: Varies
Description: Awarded to exceptional music students planning to study at the Conservatory.

Oklahoma

Oklahoma City University - Oklahoma City, OK
Name of Scholarship: Talent Scholarships
Amount: Varies
Description: Awarded to students with talents in dance performance, dance management, music, art (studio, graphic, or photography), moving arts (film production and film studies), or theatre.

Oregon

Willamette University - Salem, OR
Name of Scholarship: Music Scholarship
Amount: Varies
Description: Awarded to students with exceptional musical abilities. Recipients are not required to major in music.

Name of Scholarship: Forensics Scholarship
Amount: Varies
Description: Awarded based on debate accomplishments in high school.

Name of Scholarship: Theatre Scholarship
Amount: Varies
Description: Awarded to students who have demonstrated a serious commitment to theatre and who plan to devote a major commitment to theatre in college.

Pennsylvania

Bucknell University - Lewisburg, PA
Name of Scholarship: Arts Merit Scholarships
Amount: $2,500-$20,000 annually
Description: Awarded to study or participate in the arts including art and art history, creative writing, dance, film/media, literature, music, and theatre.

Lehigh University - Bethlehem, PA
Name of Scholarship: Performing Arts Scholarships in Instrumental Music
Amount: $3,000 renewable annually

Description: Recognizes students with exceptional musical talent. The scholarship is open to students enrolled in any major or program.

Name of Scholarship: Performing Arts Scholarships in Theatre
Amount: $3,000 renewable annually
Description: Recognizes students with exceptional talent in the theatre arts including performance, design, technical, and playwriting.

Name of Scholarship: Cutler-Sametz Choral Arts Scholarships
Amount: Varies
Description: Recognizes talented singers who are interested in joining the University Choir.

Name of Scholarship: Snyder Family Marching 97 Scholarships
Amount: $1,000-$2,500
Description: Awarded to students who demonstrate musical talent and leadership skills. Recipients are expected to participate in the marching band.

Curtis Institute of Music - Philadelphia, PA
Name of Scholarship: Curtis Institute of Music Scholarship
Amount: Full tuition
Description: Awarded to all admitted students.

Moore College of Art & Design - Philadelphia, PA
Name of Scholarship: Board of Trustees Scholarship, Presidential Scholarship, Dean's Scholarship, and Admissions Scholarship

Amount: up to $18,000 renewable annually
Description: Awarded to students who demonstrate exceptional artistic and academic ability.

Name of Scholarship: Dr. Andrea Baldeck and William M. Hollis, Jr. Scholarship in Photography & Digital Arts
Amount: up to $1,250 renewable annually
Description: Awarded to students on the basis of art portfolio excellence, academic history, financial need, and an interest in photography and digital arts.

Name of Scholarship: Evelyn Andrew Whitaker Art Endowed Scholarship
Amount: up to $1,250 renewable annually
Description: Awarded to students on the basis of art portfolio excellence, academic history, and financial need.

Name of Scholarship: Fran R. Graham '66 Endowed Scholarship
Amount: up to $1,250 awarded annually
Description: Awarded to students on the basis of portfolio excellence, academic history, financial need, and an interest in design.

Rhode Island

Roger Williams University - Bristol, RI
Name of Scholarship: Judge Thomas J. Paolino Theatre/ Arts Scholarship Fund
Amount: Varies
Description: Awarded to students who display excellence in the visual or performing arts.

Name of Scholarship: Mary J. Staab Memorial

Scholarship
Amount: Varies
Description: Awarded to students who demonstrate a strong interest in theater or dance and who have strong academic accomplishments and demonstrate financial need.

South Carolina

Furman University - Greenville, SC
Name of Scholarship: Art Department Scholarships
Amount: $1,000-$14,000 annually
Description: Awarded to students who wish to actively participate in the art department (as either majors or non-majors) based on the review of an art portfolio.

Name of Scholarship: Music Scholarships
Amount: Varies
Description: Awarded to students with exceptional music abilities (open to majors and non-majors).

Name of Scholarship: Theatre Arts Scholarships
Amount: At least $10,000 annually
Description: Awarded to students who show a commitment to theatre arts and a desire to major in theatre arts.

South Dakota

Northern State University - Aberdeen, SD
Name of Scholarship: Art Scholarships
Amount: Varies
Description: Awarded to students with exceptional art portfolios and a solid academic background.

Name of Scholarship: Music Scholarships
Amount: Varies
Description: Awarded students with exceptional music abilities. Students are not required to major in music and are selected via an audition process either in-person or by submitting a CD/DVD.

Tennessee

Belmont University - Nashville, TN
Name of Scholarship: Music Scholarships
Amount: Varies
Description: Awarded to students with musical talent who plan to major in music. Recipients are determined based on their level of musical involvement, performance at an audition, and their academic records.

Name of Scholarship: Art Scholarships
Amount: Varies
Description: Awarded to students with talents in art who plan to major in art. Recipients are determined based on a portfolio, personal interview, and their academic records.

Texas

Rice University - Houston, TX
Name of Scholarship: Trustee Distinguished Scholarship
Amount: $21,000-$24,000 renewable annually
Description: Awarded to students whose personal talents distinguish themselves within the pool of admitted applicants. Past recipients have demonstrated talents in the creative and performing arts and in writing.

Trinity University - San Antonio, TX
Name of Scholarship: Baker Duncan Scholarships
Amount: $2,000-$10,000 per semester, renewable each semester
Description: Awarded to students who have displayed talent in art, debate, theatre in music.

Name of Scholarship: Trinity Music Scholarship
Amount: $1,000-$9,000 renewable annually
Description: Awarded to both music majors and non-majors who have demonstrated exceptional musical abilities.

Name of Scholarship: Urban Debate League Scholarship
Amount: $5,000 per semester, renewable each semester
Description: Awarded to students who have been involved in competitive debate.

Utah

Westminster College - Salt Lake City, UT
Name of Scholarship: Talent Scholarships
Amount: Varies
Description: Awarded to students with talents in theatre and music based on an audition.

Vermont

Green Mountain College - Poultney, VT
Name of Scholarship: Creative Arts Scholarship
Amount: up to $5,000 annually
Description: Awarded to students with superior talent in the creative arts as demonstrated in an art portfolio, DVD, CD, or cassette submitted with one's application.

University of Richmond - Richmond, VA
Name of Scholarship: Music and Theatre/Dance Scholarships
Amount: Varies
Description: Awarded to students who demonstrate outstanding promise in the study of music or theatre/dance.

Washington

Whitman College - Walla Walla, WA
Name of Scholarship: Campbell Music Scholarships
Amount: $500-$4,000 annually
Description: Awarded by the Music Department and available to students planning to major in any field.

Name of Scholarship: The Higley Scholarship
Amount: $1,000-$8,000 annually
Description: Awarded by the Music Department to students who plan to major in music.

West Virginia

Bethany College - Bethany, West Virginia
Name of Scholarship: Marching Band/Choir Scholarship
Amount: $750
Description: Awarded to students who participate in the college band or choir.

<u>Wisconsin</u>

Lawrence University - Appleton, WI
Name of Scholarship: Music Scholarships
Amount: $15,000-$22,000 annually
Description: Awarded to students who plan on enrolling in the Conservatory of Music based on an audition.

Name of Scholarship: Music Education Scholarships
Amount: Varies
Description: Awarded to students who plan to enroll in the Conservatory of Music with an interest in the Music Education major.

Name of Scholarship: Composition Scholarships
Amount: Varies
Description: Awarded to accomplished student composers who plan to enroll in the Conservatory of Music who wish to major in Theory/Competition. Applicants are asked to submit three music stores, a statement of compositional interests and goals, and a list of compositions.

Name of Scholarship: Piano Accompanying Fellowships
Amount: Varies
Description: Awarded to highly gifted pianists who plan to enroll in the Conservatory of Music. Recipients must provide accompanying services 10 to 12 hours per week in ensembles and individual studios.

Name of Scholarship: Ensemble Awards
Amount: Varies
Description: Awarded to students with strong musical talents who are not pursuing a music degree. Students

must participate in one major ensemble.

Name of Scholarship: Ted Cloak Century Scholarship
Amount: up to $5,000 annually
Description: Awarded to students with talents in acting or design and technical theatre who plan to participate in theatre at Lawrence.

<u>Wyoming</u>

University of Wyoming - Laramie, WY
Name of Scholarship: Art Scholarships
Amount: Varies
Description: Awarded to prospective art majors with outstanding talents in the visual arts.

Chapter 29
Community Service and Leadership Scholarships

<u>Alaska</u>

University of Alaska at Fairbanks - Fairbanks, AK
Name of Scholarship: UAF Human Achievement Award
Amount: at least $2,500
Description: Awarded to students with a record of service to a community, non-profit organization, or special interest group as well as a commitment to high academic standards. Recipients must have at least a 2.5 GPA and an 18 ACT (or 1290 SAT CR+M).

<u>Arizona</u>

Arizona State University - Tempe, AZ
Name of Scholarship: Leadership Scholarship Program
Amount: Varies
Description: Awarded to students who have exhibited outstanding academic performance and leadership involvement in high school.

<u>Arkansas</u>

Hendrix College - Conway, AR
Name of Scholarship: Hendrix College Leadership

Scholarship
Value: $2,000 annually
Description: Awarded to students with a demonstrated record of leadership, activities, and honors.

Colorado

Colorado College - Colorado Springs, CO
Name of Scholarship: Leadership Scholarship
Value: $10,000 annually
Description: Awarded to students based on outstanding academic, leadership, and extracurricular achievement.

Georgia

Berry College - Mount Berry, GA
Name of Scholarship: Leadership Fellows Scholarship
Amount: $3,000-$6,000 annually
Description: Awarded to students with extraordinary leadership and service records.

Name of Scholarship: Entrepreneurship Scholarship
Amount: Varies
Description: Awarded to students who are interested in majoring or minoring in business and have an interest in being involved in the entrepreneurship program. Students should demonstrate an interest or have experience in entrepreneurship.

Name of Scholarship: Model United Nations Scholarship
Amount: Varies
Description: Awarded to students who have demonstrated significant Model UN or simulation experience. Students must be interested in joining and

competing with the Berry College Model United Nations organization.

Emory University - Atlanta, GA
Name of Scholarship: J. Pollard Turman Leadership Scholars
Amount: Full Tuition + Fees
Description: Awarded to students who show leadership potential as demonstrated by a commitment to service and excellence in school, civic, and other activities in conjunction with academic achievement. Students from all states are considered although residents of the Southeast receive special consideration.

Name of Scholarship: Robert W. Woodruff Scholars
Amount: Full Tuition + Fees
Description: Awarded to students who have demonstrated forceful and unselfish character, intellectual and personal vigor, outstanding academic achievement, impressive communication skills, significant leadership and creativity in school or the community, and clear potential to enrich student life at Emory.

Indiana

Indiana University - Bloomington, IN
Name of Scholarship: The School of Public and Environmental Affairs Selective Scholarship
Amount: $5,000 renewable annually
Description: Awarded to high-achieving students who demonstrate a strong interest in public affairs (including policy, civic engagement, sustainability, management, and promotion of the arts) and who plan to enroll in the the School of Public and Environmental Affairs.

Iowa

Cornell College - Mount Vernon, IA
Name of Scholarship: Community Enrichment Award
Value: $10,000 renewable annually
Description: Awarded to students who have contributed to their schools or communities in a meaningful way.

Kentucky

Centre College - Danville, KY
Name of Scholarship: New Horizons Scholarship
Amount: $22,000
Number of Awards: up to 40
Description: Awarded to talented students likely to provide to campus leadership in the area of diversity.

Louisiana

Tulane University - New Orleans, LA
Name of Scholarship: Community Service Scholarship
Amount: $20,000 annually
Number of Awards: 15
Description: Rewards students who have demonstrated a high level of academic achievement as well as dedication to servicing the community with leadership, passion, peer engagement, and resourcefulness.

Maryland

Goucher College - Baltimore, MD
Name of Scholarship: Dr. Rhoda M. Dorsey Leadership Scholarship

Amount: $5,000 renewable annually

Description: Recognizes students who have distinguished themselves through non-academic engagement such as special talents and extracurricular achievements with a particular focus on leadership.

Massachusetts

Babson College - Babson Park, MA
Name of Scholarship: Diversity Leadership Award
Amount: half tuition to full tuition annually
Description: Awarded to students who have demonstrated leadership in bridging differences and building inclusive communities across "individual and intersecting identities" such as race, ethnicity, religion, social class, nationality, disability, sexual preference and gender expression. Students with need can be awarded up to full tuition.

Name of Scholarship: Center for Women's Entrepreneurial Leadership Scholarship
Amount: One quarter tuition
Description: Awarded to incoming students based on academic achievement and demonstrated leadership.

Michigan

Kalamazoo College - Kalamazoo, MI
Name of Scholarship: Enlightened Leadership Award
Amount: $5,000 renewable annually
Number of Awards: 20
Description: Awarded to students with exceptional involvement in social activism and community engagement, international activism, or sustainability and

environmental activism.

Minnesota

St. Olaf College - Northfield, MN
Name of Scholarship: Service Leadership Award
Amount: $4,000-$10,000 annually
Description: Awarded to students who have demonstrated a commitment to investing in others through leadership and service to organizations and projects for the benefit of their communities.

Missouri

Washington University in St. Louis - St. Louis, MO
Name of Scholarship: Entrepreneurial Scholars Program
Amount: $3,000 renewable annually
Number of Awards: up to eight
Description: Awarded to students who possess creativity, energy, and an entrepreneurial spirit that strives to translate their visions into profit and nonprofit enterprises for the benefit of the community.

Montana

Carroll College - Helena, MT
Name of Scholarship: Carroll College Service Leadership Scholarship
Value: up to $10,000 renewable annually
Description: Awarded to high-achieving students who have a commitment to local, community, or global service. Applicants must have at least a 3.5 GPA and a 25 ACT (or SAT equivalent).

Nebraska

Doane College - Crete, NE
Name of Scholarship: Doane's Leadership Award
Value: up to $1,500 annually
Description: Awarded to students who have demonstrated leadership or who have leadership potential.

New Jersey

Drew University - Madison, NJ
Name of Scholarship: Civic Engagement Scholarship
Amount: $20,000 total ($5,000 annually)
Description: Awarded to students who have demonstrated a commitment to community service and civic engagement.

New York

Hobart and William Smith Colleges - Geneva, NY
Name of Scholarship: The Environmental Sustainability Trustee Scholarship
Amount: $25,000 annually
Description: Awarded to students with a demonstrated commitment to environmental leadership, sustainability, energy and environmental policy, climate change science or policy, or similar.

Name of Scholarship: The Edward E. Rigney '31 Scholarship in Debate
Amount: $17,000 annually
Description: Awarded to students who have significant success in the areas of Debate, Model UN or other

similar activities.

Name of Scholarship: Hersh Scholarships
Amount: Full tuition plus fees
Description: Awarded to students with a strong academic record and substantial extracurricular involvement and community service.

Ithaca College - Ithaca, NY
Name of Scholarship: Ithaca Leadership Scholar Program Award
Amount: $7,000 renewable annually
Description: Awarded to students who have a record of leadership and above average academic performance.

North Carolina

Salem College - Winston-Salem, NC
Name of Scholarship: Gramley Leadership and Service Scholarship
Amount: $14,000-$18,000 renewable annually
Description: Awarded to students who have demonstrated outstanding achievement in leadership and service.

Rhode Island

Providence College - Providence, RI
Name of Scholarship: Feinstein Scholarship
Amount: up to $5,000
Description: Awarded to students who have demonstrated a commitment to community service and who have a record of community involvement.

Name of Scholarship: Friar Scholarships
Amount: up to $9,000 annually
Number of Awards: 100
Description: Awarded to students who have displayed extraordinary commitment, leadership, and responsibility in extracurricular pursuits.

South Carolina

Furman University - Greenville, SC
Name of Scholarship: Mock Trial Scholarships
Value: Varies
Description: Awarded to students with a passion and commitment to Mock Trial and a desire to participate in Furman's Mock Trial program.

Tennessee

Belmont University - Nashville, TN
Name of Scholarship: Leadership Scholarship
Value: $2,000
Number of Awards: 25
Description: Awarded to students who have demonstrated outstanding leadership abilities.

Wake Forest University - Winston-Salem, NC
Name of Scholarship: The Hunter Family Scholarship for Community Service and the Louis Patton Hearn Scholarship for Human Service
Amount: Varies
Description: Awarded to students with strong commitments to community service.

Name of Scholarship: The Bland Scholarship for

Entrepreneurship
Amount: Varies
Description: Awarded to a student with exceptional talent in entrepreneurship.

Name of Scholarship: Lelia and David Farr Scholarship in Entrepreneurship
Amount: $5,000 annually
Description: Awarded to students who show outstanding potential in entrepreneurship and who have an interest in participating in the Program in Innovation, Creativity, and Entrepreneurship.

Texas

Rice University - Houston, TX
Name of Scholarship: Barbara Jordan Scholarship
Amount: $21,000 renewable annually
Description: Awarded to students who have distinguish themselves through initiatives that build bridges between cultural, racial, and ethnic groups.

Name of Scholarship: Trustee Distinguished Scholarship
Amount: $21,000-$24,000 renewable annually
Description: Awarded to students whose personal talents distinguish themselves within the pool of admitted applicants. Past recipients have been political and community service leaders and entrepreneurs.

University of Texas - Austin
Name of Scholarship: Rapoport Service Scholarship
Amount: $10,000 annually for three years
Description: Awarded to students interested in volunteerism, community service, and service learning.

<u>Vermont</u>

Green Mountain College - Poultney, VT
Name of Scholarship: Sustainability 2020 Award
Amount: $17,000 annually
Description: Awarded to students who have demonstrated excellence through participation in community service, leadership roles in academic and extracurricular settings, and/or dedication to environmental practices.

Name of Scholarship: Demonstrated Excellence in Environmental Practices Scholarship
Amount: $1,000 annually
Description: Awarded to students who have demonstrated a passion for the environment through academic research, community service, poetry, or art.

Chapter 30
Scholarship Resources

There are thousands of organizations that give away outside scholarships to students each year ranging from several hundred dollars to full tuition and awarding students of all kinds. The websites below host searchable databases which allow you to search for and filter scholarships that might be relevant to you.

Cappex.com
Cappex has a scholarship directory amounting to over $11 billion in scholarships. You can also use Cappex to read college reviews and compare statistics on different college options.

College Board Scholarship Search
The College Board has an easily searchable database of $6 billion worth of scholarships with an extensive filter system that easily allows you to find scholarships relevant to you.

Fastweb.com
Fastweb has a databases of 1.5 million scholarship opportunities which you can search by category. They also have a list of sweepstakes and promotions that award money for college as well as information and articles about financial aid.

Scholarships.com

Scholarships.com has a database of 2.7 million local, state, and national scholarships which you can search online.

ScholarshipExperts.com

The searchable scholarship database on ScholarshipExperts.com has over two million scholarships which award over $14 billion. The website also offers financial aid resources for students and families. They also offer their own scholarship each month which offer $1,500-$5,000 in prize money.

StudentScholarships.org

Although their website is slightly less user-friendly than some of their competitors, StudentScholarships.org claims to have the largest database of scholarships on the web.

Supercollege.com

Supercollege.com has an online database containing 2.2 million scholarships which you can access by creating a free profile.

Zinch.com

An online scholarship database, Zinch has students fill out a comprehensive profile and then matches them with scholarship opportunities. Zinch also sponsors its own scholarships giving away a weekly $1,000 award to a student who submits a three sentence essay.

Pallas Snider Ziporyn

Pallas Snider Ziporyn is a college counselor, writer, blogger, and author of *The International Student's Guide to American Colleges*. She specializes in college search and selection, financial aid, admissions to elite colleges, and applying to American universities from abroad. She is a 2010 graduate of Harvard College and while a student worked in Harvard's Office of Admissions.

Pallas lives in Vermont with her husband. For more information, visit her website at thecollegematchmaker.com.